GREAT EMPIRES OF THE PAST

Empire of the Mongols

MICHAEL BURGAN

☑®
Facts On File, Inc.

Great Empires of the Past: EMPIRE OF THE MONGOLS

HISTORY CONSULTANT: Christopher P. Atwood, professor of Mongolian History, Indiana University; editor of *Journal of the Mongolia Society*

Facts On File, Inc.
132 West 31st Street
New York NY 10001

Library of Congress Cataloging-in-Publication Data
Burgan, Michael.
Empire of the Mongols / Michael Burgan.
p. cm. – (Great empires of the past)
Includes bibliographical references and index.
ISBN 0-8160-5563-7 (alk. paper)
1. Mongols–History–Juvenile literature. I. Title. II. Series.
DS19.B87 2004
951'.025–dc22   2004028479

Facts On File books are available at special discounts when purchased in bulk quantities for businesses, associations, institutions, or sales promotions. Please call our Special Sales Department in New York at (212) 967-8800 or (800) 322-8755.

You can find Facts On File on the World Wide Web at http://www.factsonfile.com

Produced by the Shoreline Publishing Group LLC
Editorial Director: James Buckley Jr.
Series Editor: Beth Adelman
Designed by Thomas Carling, Carling Design, Inc.
Photo research by Dawn Friedman, Bookmark Publishing
Index by Nanette Cardon, IRIS

Photo and art credits: The Granger Collection, NY: 4, 10, 30, 46, 83; The Art Archive/British Library: 14; Scott Darsney/Lonely Planet Images: 17; Werner Forman/Art Resource, NY: 23; Bibliotheque Nationale, Paris, France/Bridgeman Art Library: 24, 38; Frederic J. Brown/AFP/Getty Images: 34; The Art Archive/Hermitage Museum, Saint Petersburg/Dagli Orti (A): 41, 74; Facts On File: 43, 55, 117; Corel Corp.: 50; Francoise de Mulder/Corbis: 53; Jon Spaull/Corbis: 59; Minoru Iwasaki/AP/Wide World Photos: 62; Ashmolean Museum, University of Oxford, UK/Bridgeman Art Library: 68; MPI/Hulton Archive/Getty Images: 70; The Art Archive/Bibliothèque Nationale Paris: 72; Ng Han Guan/AP/Wide World Photos: 78; Olivier Cirendini/Lonely Planet Images: 80; Enzo & Paolo Ragazzini/Corbis: 90; The Art Archive/Turkish and Islamic Art Museum Istanbul/Dagli Orti (A): 92; The Art Archive/Bodleian Library Oxford/The Bodleian Library (Pococke 400 folio 99r): 94; Michel Setboun/Corbis: 97, 110; Nik Wheeler/Corbis: 100; Roger Wood/Corbis: 106; The Art Archive/Musée des Arts Décoratifs Paris/Dagli Orti (A): 113; Dean Conger/Corbis: 115; Frederic J. Brown/AFP/Getty Images: 118

Printed in the United States of America

VB PKG 10 9 8 7 6 5 4 3 2 1

This book is printed on acid-free paper.

CONTENTS

Introduction

FOR SEVERAL THOUSAND YEARS WARRIORS ON HORSEBACK rode across central Asia, conquering nearby towns and cities. These horsemen lived on the steppes, a flat, grassy region that extends from Asia into central Europe. The riders were nomads, moving from one grazing spot to another with their herds of horses, sheep, camels, goats, and cattle. Over the centuries these nomads battled such people as the ancient Greeks, the Romans, the Persians, the Chinese, and the Arabs.

Of all the nomadic warriors of central Asia, the fiercest were the Mongols. In the 13th century, starting in their homeland of Mongolia, just north of China, the Mongols spread out to the south and west. Under the leadership of Chinggis Khan (c. 1162–1227) and his descendants, the Mongols quickly built an empire that stretched from Korea to eastern Europe–the largest continuous area of land ever controlled by one ruling family. This empire soon split into four mini-empires. The last major rulers with ties to the old Mongol empire were the Mughals of northern India, who first governed in the 16th century. They traced family ties to Chinggis Khan and the later Turko-Mongol ruler Timur (1336–1405), more commonly known in English as Tamerlane.

By the time of the Mughals, the old Mongol culture had virtually disappeared in most of the lands that once formed their empire. The Mongols had adopted the ways of the people they conquered and blended into their societies. Only in their homeland of Mongolia and a few other pockets of the eastern steppes did the traditional ways endure. This willingness to learn from conquered people and take on their culture was one of the Mongols' greatest strengths. They borrowed the best of what their former enemies had to offer in politics, art, and social structure. The Mongols'

OPPOSITE

The Great Khan
Under the leadership of Chinggis Khan and his descendants, the Mongols built the largest empire ever controlled by one family. This 16th-century Persian miniature, painted 300 years after Chinggis Khan died, attests to the lasting impact he had.

5

WHAT ARE CONNECTIONS?

Throughout this book, and all the books in the Great Empires of the Past series, you will find Connections boxes. They point out ideas, inventions, art, food, customs, and more from this empire that are still part of our world today. Nations and cultures in remote history can seem far removed from our world, but these connections demonstrate how our everyday lives have been shaped by the peoples of the past.

TURKS AND MONGOLS

Throughout this book, *Mongol* is used to describe the people of Mongolia during the time of the Mongol Empire. *Mongolian*, when it is used, refers to the modern-day people of Mongolia. In a similar way, *Turkic* or *Turk* refers to past peoples, not the current inhabitants of modern Turkey.

other major strength was their military might. They had great skills on horseback and showed tremendous discipline on the battlefield. As they conquered one land, they recruited new soldiers, then kept their ever-increasing army moving into new territories.

The World of the 12th Century

For several centuries before the rise of Chinggis Khan, the Mongols were just one of many nomadic tribes that lived on the Central Asian steppes. Different Turkic peoples ruled the steppes for a time, and the Chinese also influenced the region. The tribes of Mongolia blended with the Turks, creating what is sometimes called a Turko-Mongol culture. By the 12th century, the tribes of Mongolia included the Tatars, the Mongols, the Kereyids, the Naimans, and the Merkits.

These Mongolian tribal peoples lived on the landmass called Eurasia. This continuous stretch of land includes the greater part of two continents: Europe and Asia. At its height in the second century, Rome dominated the western half of Eurasia. At about the same time, the Han Dynasty of China was the major power in the east. By the 12th century, both these empires were long gone, and a number of smaller empires and kingdoms competed for influence in the region.

Rome's empire had split in two even before its fall in the fifth century. Western Europe then broke into many different kingdoms and principalities. The Byzantine Empire, which traced its political roots to the Romans, ruled parts of Eastern Europe. In the Middle East, a single great Islamic Empire had arisen in the seventh century. It then broke up into smaller dynastic empires. In South Asia, India had developed a great culture that was more than 3,000 years old. But by the 12th century, native Indian dynasties were losing power to outsiders. The northern part of the country eventually came under the control of Turks, who had embraced Islam. Farther east in Eurasia, two competing Chinese dynasties had developed after the fall of the Han: the Song and the Jin. A number of smaller empires, some Turkic, also competed for influence on the edges of China.

Throughout the world at this time, religion played a greater role in politics and daily life than it usually does today. Religion inspired great art. It could also fuel bloody wars. But to believers it was most important for bringing release from the suffering of this world. The two halves of Europe were divided by their religion, as each region claimed that its type of Christianity was the one true faith. Islam was dominant in the Arab world and in Persia, which had once been the home of great empires. The Islamic influence spread into Central Asia, where Turkic tribes lived. In India, Hinduism and Buddhism (both native to India) were the main religions until the Moslem conquests began, while in China, Buddhism competed with Taoism (a native Chinese religion) as the main faith. The Mongols had their own faith, but they often accepted the beliefs of the people they conquered.

The empires that dominated Eurasia in the 12th century were mostly sedentary—they were built around permanent towns and cities that focused on farming and trade. They had great wealth compared to the Mongols. But in most cases they could not match the military skill of the nomadic warriors. They also had political and religious differences that kept them from working together to fight the Mongols. Those differences made it easier for the Mongols to expand their empire.

Names of a Conqueror

The historians of the Mongols' day wrote in a variety of languages, including Persian, Chinese, Arabic, and Turkic. Modern European historians using these Asian sources translate some of the Mongol names in different ways. Chinggis Khan, for example, also appears as Jingiz, Chingiz, Cinggis, and Genghis. His grandson Khubilai Khan (1215–1294) also turns up as Kubilai, Qubilai, and Kubla, and Khan is sometimes written Qa'an or Qan. The same problem emerges with geographic names. The Mongol capital of Karakorum, for example, is also spelled Qaraqorum. Sometimes, it can make for confusing history.

The Conquests Begin

The first Mongol khan emerged toward the end of the 11th century. A little later, the Mongols battled the Tatars. The Mongol chieftain Yesugei (d. c. 1175), a relative of the first khan, killed a Tatar leader named Temüjin (d. c. 1167). Yesugei then named his newborn son after the fallen Tatar, a common practice of the day. This Mongolian boy became one of the greatest generals and leaders the world has ever known—Chinggis Khan.

As nomads, the Mongols and their neighbors often raided sedentary communities. The tribes of Mongolia also raided each other. An individual warrior in one tribe often used his family connections and a strong personality to convince other warriors to join his raiding party. Temüjin followed this path to power, and his growing army fought and defeated larger tribes. By 1206, Temüjin had united almost all the Turko-Mongol tribes of Mongolia, and he received the title of Chinggis Khan. There is some debate about what this title really means: Some scholars say it means "hard or tough ruler," others believe it means "oceanic (universal) ruler," and there are still more theories. In English, Chinggis Khan, and

CONNECTIONS >>>>>>>>>>>

An Enduring Title

The Turkic title *khan* (or variations of the word) means "prince" or "king." It was used throughout Central Asia for centuries. It is commonly used today in English when talking about the great Mongol rulers Chinggis and Khubilai, but one modern ruler also uses the name. The Aga Khan (b. 1936) is the religious leader of the Shia Imami Ismaili branch of Islam. The current Aga Khan is the 49th leader with that title. A charitable organization called the Aga Khan Development Network operates in many countries with large Islamic populations, and Pakistan is the home of Aga Khan University. Khan has also become a comon surname in Pakistan and India.

each of his successors at the head of the Mongol Empire, was sometimes called the Great Khan.

The Mongols under Chinggis had one of the most powerful armies in central Asia. As the "universal" ruler, he brought the remaining tribes under his control and then began to look beyond Mongolia's borders. This time, however, the Mongols would not merely raid the sedentary civilizations that surrounded them. Chinggis wanted to conquer and dominate all the nations around him. Almost constant attacks kept the Mongol forces strong and prevented other nations from gaining enough strength to threaten the Mongols. These wars also brought great riches to Chinggis and his family.

After Chinggis

In 1223 Chinggis returned to Mongolia, and he died there in 1227. Two years later the Mongol chieftains elected Chinggis's third son, Ögedei (1186–1241), the new Great Khan. By Mongol tradition, Chinggis's empire was divided among his four sons, though the other brothers recognized Ögedei as the Great Khan of the empire. He set up his capital at Karakorum, north of today's Arvayheer, and focused his military attention on the Jin. The ultimate Mongol victory in 1234 meant that half of East Asia's greatest civilization was under the control of nomads who historically had no use for formal education, structured government, and fine arts—all trademarks of Chinese civilization. A few years later, Korea and Tibet were added to the Mongol Empire, and Ögedei also launched the first Mongol attacks on the territory controlled by the southern Chinese Song Dynasty.

Ögedei also turned his sights to the west. His generals conquered what is today Azerbaijan, Georgia, and Armenia, then forced the rulers in what is today Turkey and Iraq to pay tribute to them. Eventually, Mongol forces took control of the western steppes that stretched beyond Russia's Volga River into Hungary. The Mongols were prepared to stay in Hungary and make it a base for further expansion into Europe, but the death of Ögedei late in 1241 changed their plans. The khan's relatives and other important leaders had to return to Karakorum to choose the next Great Khan. Just as suddenly as the Mongols had swept into Europe, they left, although a large force remained in Russia. The Russians later called the Mongols' mini-empire the Golden Horde.

The Rise of Khubilai Khan

After Ögedei's death, three of Chinggis's grandsons ruled in succession as the Great Khan. The second of these rulers, Möngke (d. 1259), strengthened Mongol rule in southwest Asia, in what is now Iran and Iraq. He also prepared for a major war with the Song, and he sent his brother Khubilai to fight in lands bordering Song Dynasty territory. Khubilai's military campaign began in 1252, and he and Möngke led the Mongol armies that invaded southern China in 1258. By this time, Khubilai ruled most of northern China for his family. After Möngke died at the front in 1259, Khubilai was chosen the next Great Khan.

While Möngke and Khubilai focused their attention on China, their relatives fought in western Asia. Möngke's brother Hülegü led an expedition into the Middle East, pushing the boundaries of the empire into what is now Syria and Israel. Hülegü had his eye on Egypt as well, but before he could invade, the death of Möngke led him to pull back most of his troops into Persia and then return to Mongolia. Just as in Eastern Europe, political changes in the empire had ended a Mongol thrust, and the Mongols never again reached that far into the Middle East.

Under Khubilai, the Mongol Empire reached its largest size. The Mongols finally defeated the Song in 1279, giving them complete control of China and reuniting it for the first time in several hundred years. As Great Khan, Khubilai, in theory, ruled over the entire empire, just as Chinggis and the other Great Khans had. In reality, however, Khubilai had direct control only over China and the surrounding lands in East Asia. Other relatives of Chinggis ruled the western regions. Khubilai founded what

CONNECTIONS >>>>>>>>>>>>

From Ordu to Horde

The English word *horde* refers to a group of Central Asian nomads. It can also mean a large crowd, particularly a potentially dangerous one. *Horde* comes from the Turko-Mongol word *ordu*, which means "palace tent," where a nomadic ruler dwelt. The ruler was surrounded by his guard, often 10,000 strong.

Imperial Hunting Party

Horses were an important part of Mongolian culture, and a key to their ability to move swiftly and decisively in military campaigns. Mongolians also hunted on horseback, as illustrated by this 13th or 14th-century Chinese painting of Khubilai Khan (center) on a hunting trip.

came to be known as the Yuan Dynasty, and his family governed China until 1368. With the great wealth he amassed through conquest, Khubilai built a splendid capital city called Khan-baliq—today's Beijing, the capital of China. One famous visitor to the city was the Italian merchant Marco Polo.

The Four Empires

While Khubilai ruled from Khan-baliq, his relatives strengthened their rule in the three other mini-empires that had developed after Chinggis's death. West of China was the Chaghatai Khanate, which was named for Chinggis's son Chaghatai (c. 1185–1242). The Mongols who ruled there are sometimes called the Chaghatayids. This khanate included Transoxiana.

North of the Chaghatai Khanate was the land of the Golden Horde. On the east, this empire bordered Khubilai's China. It stretched across central Russia and included the cities of Moscow and Kiev. The descendants of Batu (d. 1255) who governed this land lived on the steppes, collecting tribute from the Russian princes who lived in the cities.

The last of the four mini-empires was the Ilkhanate, centered in Persia and founded by Hülegü. The title Ilkhan means "lesser prince," reflecting the notion that the Great Khan was in theory still in charge of the region. The Mongols who ruled the Ilkhanate were sometimes called the Ilkhanids. Their first capital was Tabriz , in what is now Iran; Öljeitü (c. 1280–1316), a descendant of Hülegü, later moved it to nearby Sultaniyya.

Decline in the East, New Empire in the West

During the mid to late 1300s, the Mongol empire saw many changes. Khubilai's grandson Temür Öljeitü (c. 1276–1307) was the last of the Great Khans who had authority over all the Mongol lands, as the smaller khanates became more independent. Only the Ilkhanate had recognized the authority of Khubilai and his son. By the 1340s, the Ilkhanids were out of power, with their lands ruled by a series of local leaders—Arabs, Turks, Persians, and Mongols. Parts of the Chaghatai Khanate also came under local control. The Golden Horde fell into chaos in 1360, and a Russian victory at Kulikovo Pole in 1380 showed that the Russians were gaining strength.

Out of the Chaghatai Khanate, a new empire rose during the late 14th century. The driving force behind it was Timur, a Muslim Mongol from the Barulas tribe who spoke Turkish. Timur married a princess descended from Chinggis Khan and used this relationship to suggest he was a worthy successor of the first Great Khan. Like Chinggis, Timur was a brave warrior who convinced others to join his army. Timur never took the title of khan, but he tried to duplicate Chinggis's military success and build his own "Mongol" Empire.

From his base in Transoxiana, Timur spread his rule over

Marco Polo

Other Europeans reached Mongol lands before Marco Polo did and wrote about their adventures. *The Travels of Marco Polo*, however, is the most famous account of 13th-century Asia that is still widely read in the Western world. Polo, along with his father and uncle, left Venice in 1271 to visit China. He spent more than 20 years traveling through and living in the great Mongol Empire, and for a time worked in Khubilai Khan's government. Polo's description of his experience was read across Europe. Many people doubted his account, and some of his details about Chinese culture and warfare are not accurate.

A few modern historians claim that Polo never visited China at all. They say he could have gathered his facts about Khubilai and China from Arab and Persian traders. Most scholars, however, accept that Polo did travel through China. And whether he did or not, his book certainly inspired other Europeans to travel to China and other parts of East Asia. Christopher Columbus, for one, owned a copy of Polo's book. When he left on his famous voyage in 1492, Columbus hoped to reach East Asia, just as Polo had.

most of the former Ilkhanate and the western half of the Chaghatai Khanate. His lands included modern-day Iran, Iraq, Uzbekistan, Turkmenistan, and parts of Afghanistan. His troops battled the Golden Horde, Indian forces, and Ottomans–Turks who lived in what is now Turkey. Timur founded a dynasty, the Timurids, that lasted until 1507.

Timurid influence extended into northern India, where the Mughal Empire arose. The name came from Indians who believed the Mughals were descendants of Chaghatai (*Mughal* is the Persian word for *Mongol*). In reality, the founder of their dynasty, Zahiruddin Babur (1483–1530), was mostly Turkic, although he had family ties to Chinggis. Later Mughal rulers came from different ethnic groups, including Persian and Indian. Still, even if the Mughals did not follow traditional Mongol culture, they felt influenced by it, and the people they ruled remembered the dominance of Timur and the earlier Mongol khans. The Mughals ruled in northern India until the early 19th century.

The Impact of the Mongol Empire

The rise of the Mongols marked the last major clash between nomadic and sedentary cultures. The Mongols won swift victories, but over time the nomadic peoples could not compete with the wealth and knowledge created in sedentary societies. New methods of warfare gave sedentary armies a way to defeat archers on horseback. And in many parts of their empire, the people the Mongols defeated eventually had the strength to rise up against them. Still, the Mongols built a vast world empire faster than any people before or after them. They united Eurasia in a truly international trading system and encouraged new forms of communication. They demonstrated the value of religious tolerance at a time when religious differences often led to wars. The Mongols brought culture and knowledge learned from conquered peoples to all parts of their empire. They helped reduce cultural isolation among a large part of the world's population.

People living in the Western world today might not see the Mongol influence on history. They did not shape the modern Western world's language and literature, as the Greeks and Romans did. They did not create a culture that still thrives in a large part of the world, as the Arabs did. Yet, as this book will show, the Mongols do have many connections to the modern world. For one thing, Mongol rule helped unify both Russia and China–two of today's most powerful nations. No one can deny the role that one ruler–Chinggis Khan–and his family had on shaping world history.

A ROYAL NICKNAME

Timur was nicknamed Timur-i leng, which is Persian for "the lame Timur." A leg injury made him limp when he walked. Europeans turned Timur-i leng into *Tamerlane* or *Tamburlaine*, and Timur is still often called these names in English and other European languages.

PART I

HISTORY

The Rise of the Mongol Empire

Completing the Mongol Empire

Final Years of the Khanates

CHAPTER 1

The Rise of the Mongol Empire

THE TRADITIONAL HOMELAND OF THE MONGOLS SITS ON the eastern end of the central Asian steppes. To the west are the Altai and Tian Shan Mountains, with the forests of Siberia to the north. The Gobi Desert lies to the south, and to the east is the forested Greater Kuinggan Range. A few rivers cut through Mongolia, but it has no direct access to major waterways or the ocean. The steppe here is about a mile above sea level, and the climate can be harsh, with a short summer and extremely cold winter. The 13th century Italian priest Giovanni DiPlano Carpini (c. 1180–c. 1252), author of *The Story of the Mongols Whom We Call Tartars*, described the conditions he faced on his journey from 1245 to 1247 to meet the Great Khan Guyuk (d. 1248). He wrote, "We had to throw ourselves flat to the ground because of the force of the wind, and there was so much dust we could hardly see." Hail and severe thunderstorms, the priest wrote, were common.

The climate, sandy soil, and lack of a steady water supply made farming difficult for the people of the steppes. They relied on their herd animals for basic supplies, such as food and clothing. The Mongols and their nomadic neighbors moved with their flocks between summer and winter grazing areas. When they could not meet their needs through herding and hunting, they traded with the city dwellers of China and Central Asia who lived just beyond the steppes.

Early Steppe Empires

Before the rise of the Mongols, other steppe peoples created their own empires in central Asia. The Turks controlled a large part of the region in the sixth and seventh centuries. The Turks called their ruler *kaghan*, which

OPPOSITE
Unifying Force
This 1397 illustration from a Persian poem about Chinggis Khan shows him (right middle) fighting the Chinese. China was united under Mongol rule in 1279.

later became *khan*. According to historian J. J. Saunders, author of *The History of the Mongol Conquests*, the Turks were notable for being the first "barbarian" nomads to create a unified empire in the steppes. To the sedentary people of the world, the nomads were barbarians because they lacked education, formal governments, and fine arts. The Turks were also "the first barbarians to create a kingdom so extensive as to touch at different points the four great civilized societies of the day: China, India, Persia, and Byzantium," according to Saunders. (Byzantium was the remains of the eastern half of the earlier Roman Empire.) The Mongols would later repeat that feat, with the borders of their empire stretching far beyond the first great Turkic state.

After the Turkic empire collapsed during the middle of the eighth century, a Turkic people called the Uighurs emerged as the central power. Their capital was near the site of the future Mongol capital of Karakorum. The Uighurs later shaped Mongol culture: Their alphabet was used to write Mongolian, and the Uighurs developed political structures that the Mongols copied.

The tribes of Mongolia next came under the control of the Kitans, who rose to power during the early 10th century. The Kitans were nomads and spoke a language that was related to Mongolian. Coming from the north, the Kitans also took over part of China, and they introduced some elements of Chinese culture to the Mongols.

In 1115, the Jürchen rebelled against the Kitans. The Jürchen were a branch of the Manchu people, which lived in northeastern China. They were farmers like the Chinese, but rode horses and raised livestock like the Mongols. Their language was much influenced by the Mongols, as well. The rebellion went on for several years, and around 1120, the Kitans fell to the Jürchen, although some Kitans fled to the west and founded a new empire, Kara-Kitay, based in Transoxiana. As the new rulers of northern China, the Jürchen founded the Jin

CONNECTIONS >>>>>>>>>>>>

Early Asian Invaders

The Turks of the seventh century were following an old tradition of nomadic warriors coming into contact with more civilized peoples to the west. In the fifth century, the Huns rode across the steppes and attacked parts of the crumbling Roman Empire. Many historians believe the Huns were descendants of the Xiongnu, a people who first lived in Mongolia. The most famous Hun in European history is Attila, who led an invading force that reached Paris. The name Attila the Hun is still used today to refer to someone who is especially brutal, and the country Hungary gets its name from the Huns, who once lived there.

Dynasty. When the Jürchen overthrew the Kitan rulers, the Mongols broke away. This decision led to the rise of independent chieftains within Mongolia, but they still recognized the Jürchen as their ultimate rulers.

The Mongols Before Chinggis Khan

Through centuries of war in Central Asia, the people of Mongolia mostly kept to themselves, living as herders. The Mongols were just one of the tribes there, along with other peoples of Mongolian and Turkic ethnic backgrounds. The various tribes often married women from other tribes. This interaction created the Turko-Mongolian culture. The tribes were also influenced by the various outsiders who ruled the region.

The Mongols may have first come to Mongolia from the forests of Siberia. By the 12th century, different Mongol clans had formed tribes, each led by a great warrior. Members of a tribe were often related, but just as important was a bond called an *anda*. In this relationship, two unrelated men promised their loyalty to one another and acted as if they were related. Men also chose to serve under certain leaders, giving up their ties to their family in the process. A man who made this commitment to a leader was called a *nökör*.

Under the Jin, the Tatars were probably the most influential tribe in Mongolia, since they were allied with the Jin leaders. The Tatars were also traditional enemies of the Mongols, and the two tribes often clashed. *The Secret History of the Mongols* is the only known Mongolian source for the history of this era (its author is unknown). It describes how "13 times they [the Mongols] joined battle with . . . the Tatar." During one of these battles, a Mongol chieftain named Yesugei killed a Tatar named Temüjin. Yesugei then named his newborn son after his dead enemy–a common practice at the time.

Nomadic Herders
Modern Mongolian herders drive a pack of horses on the steppes. The nomadic way of life has been part of Mongol culture for 1,000 years.

Yesugei and his son Temüjin were related to Mongol nobles, yet by the time Yesugei was born, his family did not wield great power. When Temüjin was nine, his father died, making Temüjin the leader of his tribe. The men who had served under Yesugei did not want to follow a boy, so they deserted him. Temüjin and his family spent several years on their own, barely able to survive. Finally, when Temüjin was about 16 years old, he made several important alliances. First he recruited other warriors to serve him as *nökörs* (men who chose to serve under certain leaders, giving up their ties to their family in the process). Temüjin then united with Toghril (d. 1203), the leader of the Kereyid tribe of Mongolia. Toghril and Temüjin's father had once been *anda* to each other. With this alliance, the Mongols and the Kereyids defeated the Tatars, who by this time had lost favor with the Jin. Temüjin eventually emerged as the supreme Mongol leader. His troops defeated the other tribes of Mongolia, and in 1206 the chieftains held a meeting called a *quriltai*. The Mongol leaders gave Temüjin the title Chinggis Khan.

The 13th-century Persian historian Juzjani (1193–1265) described Chinggis's appearance and attitude (as quoted by J. J. Saunders in *The History of the Mongol Conquests*): The Great Khan was "a man of tall stature, of vigorous build, robust in body, the hair on his face scanty and turned white, with cat's eyes, possessed of great energy, discernment, genius and understanding, awe-inspiring, a butcher, just, resolute, an overthrower of enemies, intrepid . . . and cruel."

Chinggis's First Conquests

Chinggis was determined to use his military strength to conquer neighboring lands. He believed he had been chosen by the Mongolian god, Eternal Heaven, to rule the world. The Mongols believed in many spirits that ruled their herds, the success of the hunt, and almost all other aspects of their lives. But the right to rule was granted by Eternal Heaven only. They believed there was just one ruler in heaven, and just one on earth—Chinggis Khan.

There were also political reasons for Chinggis's military actions. He insisted neighboring rulers hand over all refugees fleeing from Mongol rule. If they harbored these refugees, they were considered hostile nations.

Chinggis's first attack came in 1209, as the Mongols invaded Xixia, in what is now northwest China, south of the Gobi Desert. The Tanguts, most likely from Tibet, ruled this empire, which had once been part of China. Rather than face a superior military force, the Tangut rulers quickly

THE ROOTS OF A TRIBAL FEUD

The troubles between the Mongols and the Tatars increased at a time when Ambaghai (12th century) ruled as khan of the Mongols. Ambaghai hoped to improve relations with the Tatars by marrying one of his daughters to a Tatar leader. Another Tatar clan, however, kidnapped Ambaghai while he and his daughter traveled to the wedding. The Tatars took their captive to the Jin rulers, who killed him. According to *The Secret History of the Mongols*, Ambaghai sent his people a message before he died: "Till the nails of your five fingers disappear through wear; till your ten fingers are worn away through rubbing, strive to avenge me."

agreed to pay tribute to Chinggis and accept his rule. With Xixia now united with Mongolia, Chinggis controlled a key section of the Silk Road, a major trade route across Asia. He also had a western route for his troops when they attacked the Mongols' major threat in the east, the Jin.

The invasion of northern China began in 1211. At first the Mongols were content merely to loot Jin cities and then return home, but eventually they took control of their enemies' lands. In 1215 the Mongols captured the Jin's northern capital, Yanjing (the site of modern-day Beijing), forcing the Jin rulers to flee south. Despite that loss the Jin continued to fight, and the war with the Mongols dragged on for another 19 years.

On the open plains of the steppe, the Mongols were nearly invincible. They could ride their horses for days and shoot arrows as they rode. They relied on their speed and discipline to catch their enemies off guard. Their army was split into divisions of 10,000 soldiers, called *tumens*, which were further broken down into 10 *migghans*. Each of these *migghans* had 10 squadrons, or *ja'uns*, with 100 men. Chinggis often had *tumens* travel separately, then skillfully brought them together at the right time and place for battle.

Deception was also key, as the Mongols sometimes faked attacking from one direction while their main force prepared to attack from another direction. Chinggis would also have his men pretend to retreat to lure their enemy into following them. Then the retreating forces would maneuver the enemy into a position where hidden Mongols could easily defeat them.

The Mongols' usual cavalry tactics, however, did not work well in crowded cities, and in China they had to adopt new methods of waging war. Using the skills of captured Chinese engineers, they built siege engines. These included different kinds of catapults, which hurled rocks and flaming or explosive objects. Siege warfare involved cutting off a city from the outside world so it could not receive supplies or fresh troops. The Mongols tried to force their urban enemies to surrender, while using the siege

CONNECTIONS >>>>>>>>>>>

Outflanking the Enemy

A key part of Mongol military strategy was flanking, or coming at an enemy from the side instead of head on. The Mongols' mobility on their horses made this strategy work, along with their deception tactics. The different army units used flags and torches to communicate with each other as they maneuvered into a flanking position. Into modern times, generals around the world have studied the tactics of Chinggis and the other great Mongol generals, replacing horses with tanks and other gasoline-powered vehicles.

engines to wear down their defenses. For decades to come, the Mongols combined their cavalry attacks with siege warfare. The adoption of siege warfare was what made the Mongols different from other nomadic empires and is an important reason they grew so powerful.

Fighting in the West

In 1218, Chinggis turned his attention to Kara-Kitay, west of the Altai Mountains. A defeated tribal chieftain named Küchülüg (d. 1218) had fled there from Mongolia after Chinggis rose to power. Küchülüg managed to take control of Kara-Kitay, and Chinggis feared he might assemble an army that could threaten the Mongols. A Mongol force of about 20,000 men invaded Kara-Kitay. The people welcomed them, since Küchülüg had killed a local prince and limited the practice of Islam, the major faith in that area. Kara-Kitay quickly fell to the Mongols.

The growing Mongol Empire now bordered Khorazm, a Muslim empire that stretched from the Caspian Sea to Transoxiana and south into what is now Afghanistan. Its ruler was Sultan Muhammad, who was also called Khorazm-shah (d. 1220). In 1218, he provoked Chinggis by refusing to punish a Khorazmian governor who had killed hundreds of Mongol merchants. The governor believed the merchants' trading expedition contained spies—which it most likely did, as Chinggis wanted to know the military strengths and weaknesses of his neighbors. One Mongol survived the attack and reported back to Chinggis. The angry Great Khan then sent three ambassadors to Sultan Muhammad, demanding that he punish the governor who ordered the massacre. The Khorazmian ruler not only refused, he murdered one of the ambassadors. Chinggis said, "The Khorazm-shah is no king, he is a bandit," (quoted by Paul Ratchnevsky in *Genghis Khan: His Life and Legacy*). The Great Khan then prepared his troops for their first major war in the west.

By the spring of 1219, Chinggis had amassed an army of about 200,000 soldiers. His forces included Uighurs and Karluks, an ethnic group from Kara-Kitay, all split into three main sections. The Khorazmians had a larger army composed of Muslim Turks and Persians. Sultan Muhammad, however, did not want to meet the Mongols on the open battlefield, because he was not sure how to confront a three-pronged threat. The Khorazmian ruler also doubted the loyalty of his troops. Most of them were Turks who favored his mother over him. Sultan Muhammad did not trust them to obey his orders, and they did not work well with the Persians in the army. The sultan kept his forces stationed in the various cities of the

TRANSOXIANA

During the Mongol era, the region of Transoxiana was the site of many battles. The name comes from the Oxus River—called Amu Darya in Arabic—and means "beyond the Oxus." The Oxus starts in the Hindu Kush mountains in a region bordered by modern China, India, Tajikistan, and Afghanistan. Transoxiana included land west and north of the river in the heart of Central Asia. The region's many rivers enabled farmers to irrigate crops and led to the development of several key cities, such as Samarkand and Bukhara, located in modern Uzbekistan.

empire, where they became easy targets for the Mongols. Chinggis and his youngest son Tolui (1193–1233) led the attack on the major city of Bukhara before heading to the capital of Samarkand.

In perhaps one of the deadliest wars in history, the Mongols slaughtered hundreds of thousands of Khorazm soldiers and civilians. Historians of the day put the death toll in the millions. The Arab historian Ibn al-Athir (1160–1233) wrote (as quoted by David Morgan in *The Mongols*), "a tremendous disaster such as [this] had never happened before. . . . It may well be that the world from now until its end . . . will not experience the like of it again." Most modern historians doubt the high death toll reported in the traditional sources. Still, no one doubts that the conquest of Khorazm was brutal. In each city, the Mongols took all the valuables they could find, destroyed the protective walls, and slaughtered thousands of Khorazmian soldiers. In Bukhara, Chinggis told the people (as noted by James Chambers in *The Devil's Horsemen*), "It is your leaders who have committed these crimes, and I am the punishment of God."

In 1221 two Mongol generals, Jebe and Subedei (1176–1248), pursued Sultan Muhammad's son as he fled from the advancing enemy. The generals did not catch him, but they did scout out part of the Russian steppes. The Mongols moved northward through Georgia into Russia, passing by the Sea of Azov and then along the Volga River. Jebe and Subedei eventually met up with the main Mongol army along the Jaxartes River, on the eastern edge of Khorazm. By this time, in 1223, Chinggis had defeated the Khorazmians and was slowly making his way back to Mongolia.

The Second Great Khan

In 1226, Chinggis Khan led a second attack against the Tanguts of Xixia, because they were resisting Mongol rule. After this successful campaign, Chinggis died in 1227. He was buried in a secret location near Mongolia's Onon and Kerulen Rivers.

Using the Enemy

As he took prisoners, Chinggis dressed some of them as Mongols and had them march under Mongol banners ahead of the real Mongols during the next battle. This strategy made the Mongol army look bigger than it was, and lured enemy troops into wasting time and energy fighting the prisoners, rather than the Mongols themselves. The Mongols, however, did not use all prisoners this way. Some were allowed to buy their freedom, while skilled craftspeople were always spared, and were kept to work for the army or were sent back to Mongolia.

As Chinggis wanted, control of the empire passed to Ögedei, his third son. Ögedei's brothers and nephews (the sons of his dead brother Jochi) also received territory, called *ulus*, that they controlled. Tolui received the traditional Mongol homelands; Chaghatai controlled Transoxiana and nearby lands in Central Asia; Jochi's sons, Orda and Batu, received the steppes of what is now southern Russia, even though the western end of this area was not yet under Mongol control. In Chinggis's mind, Eternal Heaven had given him and his family all the world to control. It was only a matter of time before they ruled them. Ögedei also had his own *ulus*, composed of parts of Russia and China, as well as his authority as Great Khan over the rest of the empire. Chinggis's brothers also received small *ulus* in the northeast corner of the empire.

A *quriltai* in 1229 confirmed Ögedei as the second Great Khan. Within two years, he focused the Mongols' military might on the Jin. According to *The Secret History of the Mongols*, the Mongols "assault[ed] their towns and cities in every quarter," and looted the Jin's "gold and silver, satins having gold and having patterns, possessions, *alasas* [horses] and little slaves. . . ." By 1234, the land once controlled by the Jin Dynasty was completely under Mongol rule.

Expanding the Empire

In 1235, Ögedei called a meeting of his relatives and *nökörs* at the new Mongol capital of Karakorum. The Mongols were preparing to fight on several fronts. In the southwest, Chaghatai wanted to strengthen Mongol control over the lands Chinggis had conquered almost 15 years before. In the east, Ögedei sought to extend the empire into Song China. And the general Subedei supported Batu's call for a new campaign in Russia, which could eventually take the Mongols into Europe.

The advance into the Russian steppes was the Mongols' next major military action. Batu and Subedei led the campaign, with the general providing most of the strategy. Starting in the spring of 1236, Batu began assembling his army, with Ögedei's help. The commanders featured several of Chinggis's grandsons, including Berke (d. 1267), Batu's brother; Ögedei's son Guyuk; and Tolui's son Möngke. The army eventually had about 150,000 soldiers, which included Mongols, Turks, and other residents of the empire, with Chinese and Persian engineers building siege engines and other weapons of war.

The Mongols' first targets were the peoples who lived along the Volga River. Subedei's forces destroyed the Bulghars, while Möngke

A ROYAL HONOR

To honor Chinggis Khan after his death, the Mongols killed 40 slave girls and 40 horses and buried them near his grave. Mongol warriors were often buried with their horses, showing how important the animals were to them. Chinggis had ordered that his burial place be kept secret. A legend says that all the people who saw the funeral were killed, so they could never reveal the site of the Great Khan's grave.

attacked the Kipchak nomads, a numerous Turkic people who lived on the steppes from Kazakhstan to Romania. When the Mongols captured the Kipchak ruler, he refused to bow down to Möngke. The Mongol prince then ordered that the ruler's body be split in two. The lands controlled by Batu and his Golden Horde were sometimes called the Kipchak Khanate. Batu centered his forces in the Kipchaks' former homeland, where he founded his capital of Saray, near present-day Leninsk, Russia.

In Russia, the Mongols faced a series of small states ruled by princes. The first principality to fall was Riazan. Inside the city, the Mongols showed particular cruelty. They cut off all the limbs of one prince and speared some residents with large wooden stakes, leaving them to die. In *The History of the Mongol Conquests*, J. J. Saunders quotes a Russian writer who described similar brutality in nearby Kolomna, where "no eye remained open to weep for the dead." The Mongols hoped tales of their violence would spread to the other Russian principalities, so that they would surrender without a fight.

Some of the princes, however, were willing to combat the Mongols. Such key cities as Suzdal, Vladimir, and Kiev resisted, but the Mongols swept through them on their march west. As the Mongols advanced, drummers on camels beat a rhythm, and the sounds of marching animals and shouting soldiers filled the air. Although the Russians resisted, they were unwilling to unite against the superior army of their common enemy. Their ruling princes had often argued with one another and competed for power. The threat of defeat did not end these quarrels, and the Mongols controlled the Russian cities by the winter of 1240.

In some places, the Mongols completely destroyed Russian cities and the people who lived there. Father Giovanni DiPlano Carpini, in his

A Prayer for Victory
In this illustrated Moghul book (c. 1590) History of the Mongols, *Chinggis Khan (top left) prays to the sun on the Kipchak steppes before battle.*

account of the Mongols, noted that when he traveled through Kiev several years after the Mongol invasion, it was "reduced to almost nothing." The priest also described seeing "countless human skulls and bones from the dead scattered over the field." Some modern historians, however, say that some Russian cities escaped the Mongol assault or managed to rebuild soon after the Mongols moved on.

The Mongol Army

The Mongols' military success reflected a combination of several factors. The generals continued to use the tactics Chinggis had developed during his conquests, including the use of both cavalry and siege warfare. They kept the army large by forcing defeated peoples to provide soldiers. The Mongols also had a culture that greatly valued horseback riding and archery—skills that translated well from the hunting ground to the battlefield.

Almost as soon as they could walk, Mongol boys learned how to ride. After the age of 20, they were expected to fight whenever the khan ordered. By then, they had learned how to shoot while on horseback. A Mongol soldier carried two bows—one for long-range shooting and another for

Warriors on Horseback
This 13th-century illustration from a book by Rashid al-Din (an advisor to the Ilkhanate and a historian) shows Chinggis Khan (right center, on the dark horse) in battle. The Mongols could ride their horses for days and shoot arrows as they rode.

short distances—along with at least 60 arrows. With his larger bow, a warrior could shoot an arrow more than 350 yards. The Mongols used a variety of arrows, including some that carried tiny grenades. Although they preferred the bow and arrow, the Mongols also sometimes fought with swords and lances.

The Mongols used both light and heavy cavalry. The light wore lighter armor—usually made of leather—or none at all, while the heavy cavalry wore leather and mail, a protective suit made of metal. The soldiers also wore helmets—leather for the light cavalry and iron for the heavy. All soldiers carried a shield made of wicker and leather. They also carried essential supplies in their saddlebags, including food, extra clothing, and tools to repair their weapons.

CONNECTIONS >>>>>>>>>>>>

Przhevalsky's Horse

The horses the Mongols rode may be distant relatives of the only true wild horses known today—Przhevalsky's horses. (The wild horses living in the American West are actually descendants of domesticated horses brought to the Americas by the Spanish.) Their name comes from the 19th-century Russian explorer Nikolai Przhevalsky, who found a herd of them near modern Mongolia. Smaller than today's domestic horses, these wild horses once roamed the steppes near the Altai Mountains. By the 20th century, the only known Przhevalsky's horses left on Earth were in captivity. In recent years, however, Mongolian scientists have been releasing some into the wild in two of Mongolia's national parks.

The Mongol soldier's constant companion was his horse. Long before the Mongols arrived in Central Asia, the people of the steppes had tamed wild horses, then selectively bred them so they would be strong enough to carry a rider. The invention of the stirrup around 400 can be traced to the Chinese, and it quickly spread to the Asian steppe dwellers. With that simple innovation, riders could stay on their horses without using their hands, making it easier to wage war on horseback. The Mongols perfected cavalry warfare, and their culture highly valued the horse. Each soldier had several horses, rotating among them so they stayed fresh on the long rides across the steppes. The Mongols usually rode geldings—castrated male horses; riding a mare was viewed as unmanly. During desperate times, a soldier would nick his horse's skin while riding and drink some of its blood. This way, the Mongols nourished themselves without losing any speed.

Farther into Europe

Geographers usually mark the dividing line between Asia and Europe as the Ural Mountains, so with their Russian invasion, the Mongols had extended their empire into a new continent. But the push westward was not over, and by the end of 1240 the Mongols were ready to cross the Carpathian Mountains and enter Hungary. Batu and Subedei led this advance, while Baidar (dates unknown) and Kadan (dates unknown), two grandsons of Chinggis Khan, moved into Poland with a smaller force.

Early in 1241, the northern Mongol army crossed the frozen Vistula River and began attacking Polish cities. This army was trying to draw European forces out of Hungary, to pave the way for Subedei's attack. Baidar swept through Krakow, which was then the Polish capital. The residents had already fled, and the Mongols burned the city. The Mongols continued through Poland, crossing the Oder River and reaching as far as Liegnitz. At the battle outside that city, the Mongols cut off the ears of their defeated enemy, taking enough to fill nine bags. Baidar and Kadan then turned south to join the main Mongol army in Hungary.

In April 1241, the Mongols launched their attack from four directions, surrounding the Hungarian forces. They soon reached the towns of Buda and Pest (which are today united in one city along the Danube River, Budapest, and serve as Hungary's capital). The Mongols then sent scouts ahead into Austria, and one *tumen* prepared to go to Zagreb, the capital of modern Croatia. Rulers even farther west in Europe feared they might be the Mongols' next victims. By the end of 1241, Europeans had heard the reports of the Mongols' extreme violence. The reports included falsehoods—that the Mongol soldiers ate the flesh of their dead enemies, for example—but the truth was bad enough.

However, the further conquest of Europe never came. Early in 1242, Batu learned that Ögedei had died. He gathered his troops in Hungary and began the long ride back to Mongolia, to attend the *quriltai* that would choose the next Great Khan. The Mongol threat to Eastern and Central Europe was largely over, and they never again launched another major invasion there.

Unrest in the Royal Family

Chinggis's descendants took four years to choose their next leader. During that time, Ögedei's wife, Toregene (d. c. 1246), served as regent, or temporary ruler—an old Mongol custom. Ögedei had wanted his grandson Shiremün (d. c. 1251) to become the next Great Khan, but his wife favored her son Guyuk. Toregene managed to secure her son's election despite opposition from Batu, who had quarreled with Guyuk during the Russian campaign.

THE GREAT HUNT

Chinggis Khan continued the nomad tradition of training his troops based on hunting techniques. During these "great hunts," thousands of soldiers rode through an area searching for game, driving the animals out of their hiding places. Some of the troops would ride ahead until they reached a line that had been marked out in advance. They would then ride back toward the main army and the animals, creating a circle that eventually tightened around the game. The hunted animals included wolves, wild boars, and tigers. Once the soldiers had completely surrounded the animals, they killed them, providing food for an army on the march.

Carpini arrived at Karakorum in 1246, just as Guyuk was elected Great Khan. The Italian priest noted how Mongol princes and ambassadors from other nations were there to honor Guyuk, bringing him lavish gifts. Carpini wrote, "[T]here was a particular provincial governor who gave many camels to him . . . and many armored horses and mules . . . More than 50 wagons were placed beyond a hill . . . and they were all filled with gold and silver and silk clothing which were divided between the emperor and his nobles."

After the festivities of that day, the tension between the cousins Guyuk and Batu continued, and in 1247 the Great Khan prepared to attack Batu's forces. Tolui's wife, Sorkhagtani Beki (d. 1252), warned Batu about Guyuk's advance, but the civil war within the Chinggisid family never took place. Before he could launch his assault on Batu, Guyuk died in 1248. For three years his wife served as regent. During this time, Sorkhagtani wanted one of her sons to take control. Working with Batu, who did not want to become Great Khan, she convinced the Mongol princes in 1251 to choose her son Möngke as the next Mongol leader. For the next century, all the Great Khans came from the Toluid line of Chinggis's family.

The family turmoil, however, was not over. Möngke was elected at a *quriltai* held outside of Mongolia. Ögedei's and Chaghatai's families said the election was not valid, since it had not occurred in the traditional homelands. These relatives then battled Möngke and his supporters for control of the empire. Möngke won this struggle for power, and he executed many of the commanders who had helped the families of Ögedei and Chaghatai. Ögedei's son Shiremün was also executed for his role in the revolt. Tensions between the various branches of Chinggis's family lasted for decades.

Back to Persia

Möngke's first goal was to strengthen and expand Mongol control in the Islamic lands of southwest Asia. His brother Hülegü took command of a

CONNECTIONS >>>>>>>>>>>>

The Sack of Krakow

According to Polish tradition, on March 24, 1241, a Mongol arrow killed a Polish lookout in the tower of the Krakow town hall just as he was blowing an alarm on his trumpet to warn of the Mongol advance. Today Krakow still honors that event. Every hour, a trumpeter stands in the highest tower at the Church of Saint Mary and plays a simple melody that was played in medieval times as a warning call. He plays it four times, facing the four corners of the world, and each time the tune ends abruptly, just as it did for that watchman on March 24. Since 1927, this trumpet call has been broadcast on Polish radio every day at noon.

major army. As usual, the army included foreigners, such as Chinese engineers and weapons specialists who manned crude flamethrowers. These weapons fired a chemical called naphtha that was lit and then burned any flammable surface it touched. By this time, the Mongols were also using gunpowder to fire some arrows out of tubes–another technique they learned from the Chinese, and a first crude step on the road to modern rockets.

Hülegü's army crossed the Oxus River in 1256, and its first targets were the castles of the Ismailis, in parts of what are now Iran and Afghanistan. The Ismailis were extreme Shiites (Shiite is one of the two major groups in Islam; the other is Sunni). The Ismailis followed their own Shiite beliefs, and were viewed as heretic by the Sunnis, whose rulers put them under a death sentence. The Ismailis believed assassination was a legitimate way to defend themselves against this ruling. Other Muslims feared the Ismailis, and one source suggests a Muslim religious leader actually asked the Mongols to attack them. William of Rubruck (c. 1210–c. 1270), a Christian priest who visited Mongol lands, claimed Hülegü's attack was in response to a failed Ismaili plot to kill the Great Khan.

The grand master, or leader, of the Ismailis was a young man named Rukn-ad-Din (d. c. 1257). Afraid of the Mongols' might, he surrendered to Hülegü after a short siege and convinced other Ismailis to give up without a fight. Rukn-ad-Din begged Hülegü to spare his life and let him meet Möngke. The Mongol general agreed, but the Great Khan refused to meet Rukn-ad-Din, and his Mongol guards killed Rukn-ad-Din and his family.

The Drive West

Hülegü's army then continued west, heading for Baghdad. For centuries, this city in what is now Iraq had been a center of Islamic culture and politics. Its ruler was called a caliph. A caliph was both a political and religious leader, and he had great authority. The Abbasid caliphate, or kingdom, based in Baghdad had been founded in 750, and at its peak the Abbasid Dynasty controlled an empire that stretched from North Africa to Afghanistan.

In 1257, the caliph was Mustasim (d. 1258), whom historian J. J. Saunders in *The History of the Mongol Conquests* calls "weak, vain, incompetent and cowardly." Hülegü advised Mustasim to avoid a slaughter and accept Mongol rule. The caliph refused, insulted the Mongol commander, and told him to leave. Instead, Hülegü launched a typical Mongol attack from several directions, with the aid of troops from the Golden

Horde. Early in 1258, Mustasim surrendered, and the Mongols sacked Baghdad. Hülegü later wrote that his forces killed 200,000 Muslims during the battle.

Hülegü remained in Baghdad for about one year, then prepared to move west again. His ultimate goal this time was Egypt, then ruled by the Mamluks–Turkic warriors who had seized power from the caliph. By now, some Christian rulers who had been battling the Muslims in the Middle East welcomed the Mongols, even though a few decades before the no-madic raiders had attacked Christian kingdoms with equal ferocity. During the Crusades, the Christian rulers of Europe tried to push the Muslims out of the Holy Land in what is today the Middle East–the region where Jesus Christ lived and died. By the time the Mongols reached the region, only a few Christian forces remained. Some of those troops united with the Mongols against the Muslims of Syria. Others, however, refused to join the "pagan" Mongols, even against their most bitter enemy.

The Mongols took the Syrian cities of Aleppo and Damascus, and they seemed prepared to establish permanent rule throughout Syria on their way to Egypt. The Mamluks, however, staged a counterattack and won a victory at Ayn Jalut, in modern Israel, in September 1260. By this time, the Mongol army was not at full strength. Hülegü had pulled some of his forces back into Persia after learning that Möngke had died in 1259. Hülegü would have to return to Karakorum for the *quriltai* that would choose the next Great Khan. The situation paralleled the events of 1241, when the death of Ögedei had ended the Mongol thrust into Europe. Hülegü also realized that keeping a Mongol presence in the Middle East would be hard, since the region lacked grazing lands for their horses. Still, the Mongols would try to retake Syria several more times in the decades to come.

A ROYAL EXECUTION

When the Mongols killed Mustasim, they first rolled him up in a carpet, then trampled him with their horses. This or similar forms of execution were commonly used for roy-alty. The Mongols believed the blood of important people should not touch the ground.

CHAPTER 2

Completing the Mongol Empire

WHILE HÜLEGÜ BATTLED IN THE WEST, MÖNGKE FOCUSED on extending Mongol rule over the Song Dynasty territory in southern China. He died after a battle in 1259 from a fever caused by disease, not a war wound. By this time, his brother Khubilai had emerged as the major Mongol ruler in China, and Möngke let him rule part of that country. Khubilai built a capital in Kaiping, which was later renamed Shangdu–Chinese for "upper capital." The city was about 125 miles northwest of Beijing in what is now Inner Mongolia.

After Möngke's death, Khubilai and another brother, Ariq Böke (d. 1266), competed for the title of Great Khan. Ariq Böke had remained in the traditional Mongol homelands and he had the support of Mongol princes who distrusted the influence Chinese culture had had on Khubilai. Berke, the new leader of the Golden Horde, favored Ariq Böke; so did many of Chaghatai's and Ögedei's descendants. Khubilai's main supporters were his brother Hülegü and Mongol princes in China. Those princes urged Khubilai to become the Great Khan and voted for him at a *quriltai* held at Shangdu in May 1260. Ariq Böke and his supporters protested the election, and the next month Ariq Böke claimed the title of Great Khan, setting the stage for another civil war.

Ariq Böke selected generals to raise troops north and south of the Gobi Desert. These forces headed for Shangdu while Khubilai was fighting the Song in Ezhou (modern Wuhan), along the Yangtze River. The approaching threat forced Khubilai to withdraw from Ezhou and defend his capital. Ariq Böke tried to trick his older brother by assuring Khubilai that he would not attack, while simultaneously increasing his military strength. Thanks to help from a cousin, Khubilai was able to cut off Ariq Böke's

OPPOSITE
The Emperor of China
Khubilai Khan, shown here in a Yuan Dynasty Chinese painting, founded that dynasty and eventually adopted many Chinese customs and beliefs.

CONNECTIONS >>>>>>>>>>>>

From Shangdu to Xanadu

In 1816 the English writer Samuel Taylor Coleridge (1772–1834) published "Kubla Khan," a poem about Khubilai. The poem described the Great Khan's palace at Shangdu, which Coleridge called Xanadu. Since then, *Xanadu* has been used to suggest any place that is magical or filled with riches, and it was the title of a 1980 film.

forces from their supply route, limiting their ability to fight. Still, Ariq Böke was determined to confront Khubilai. The armies of the two brothers met at the end of 1261 along the Chinese-Mongol border, with neither side winning decisively.

Ariq Böke then headed into Central Asia seeking allies, allowing Khubilai to take complete control over Mongolia. Although Ariq Böke eventually won some battles, he could not compete with Khubilai's better-equipped army. In 1264, Ariq Böke finally accepted his brother's rule as Great Khan. Khubilai then killed some of the Mongols who had supported Ariq Böke, though he did not execute his brother. Instead, in 1265, Khubilai called a *quriltai* to decide what should be Ariq Böke's punishment for his civil war. Before the Mongols could meet, Ariq Böke died in 1266, under suspicious circumstances. Some historians believe he may have been poisoned, but the sources are not clear.

From then on Khubilai was unchallenged as the Great Khan. Despite his title, Khubilai had direct control only over China, Tibet, and Korea, as well as loyalty from the Mongol rulers in Persia. The rulers of the regional khanates asserted their independence in the years to come.

Khubilai Khan in China

With the defeat of Ariq Böke, Khubilai Khan focused on defeating the Song and uniting China under his rule. Conquest would extend Mongol control and improve Khubilai's image among relatives and princes who still doubted he was the true Great Khan. At the same time, he had to convince his Chinese subjects that he was worthy to rule their great civilization. As a Mongol, Khubilai was considered a barbarian. He tried to soften that image by adopting Chinese habits and customs.

Khubilai's advance into Song lands had two goals. The southern region had better farmland than the north, so it could provide the empire with food. In addition, it had sea ports that could help boost foreign trade. Khubilai also feared that if he did not unify China under his rule, the Song would eventually raise an army and try to oust their foreign rulers.

Fighting in the south presented problems the Mongol army had not faced before. The climate was hot and wet, covered in jungles, forests, and farmlands, compared to northern China and the steppes, which were cold, dry, and open. The south had few open fields where the Mongols' horses could graze. The Song were also oriented toward the sea and had a powerful navy. To defeat them, the Mongols had to build their own ships, with help from the Chinese already under their rule and other subjects with experience on the seas.

At first, Khubilai sent diplomats to ask the Song emperor to recognize his authority and avoid a war. The emperor rejected this, and in the early 1260s small battles broke out along the border between the Song and Mongol China. The first major battle took place in 1265, in the province of Sichuan, and the Mongols won. Still, the Song were determined to keep their independence, and the war dragged on for more than a decade. The Mongols staged sieges at several cities, including Xianyang, where the Mongols used thousands of boats to fight on the Yellow River. The siege of Xianyang lasted for two years. In 1276, the Mongols took over the Song capital of Hangzhou, and within three years they established complete control over southern China.

During these years of war, Khubilai officially proclaimed himself emperor of China. He gave his dynasty a Chinese name—something most foreign rulers of China did to seem less foreign. Khubilai's dynasty was called the Yuan, meaning "the origin." His government included a mixture of Chinese, Mongol, and foreign advisors. As emperor, Khubilai ruled over perhaps 65 million Chinese, while the Mongol population was only a few million.

The Great Khan made a major change in the Chinese government. In the past, most government functions were handled by civil servants. These government workers got their jobs by passing an exam. This system was designed

CONNECTIONS >>>>>>>>>>>>

A New Capital

Soon after Khubilai Khan defeated Ariq Böke, he moved the Mongol capital from Karakorum to the former northern Jin capital of Zhongdu. Khubilai renamed it Daidu, which means "great capital" in Chinese. The Turks called the city Khan-baliq, or "the khan's city." When Marco Polo traveled through China, he heard this Turkish name as Cambaluc, which is how Europeans referred to the city for centuries. In his *Travels*, Polo described Cambaluc: ". . . up and down the city there are beautiful palaces, and many great and fine [inns], and fine houses in great numbers." Today, Khubilai's capital is the Chinese capital of Beijing, and one shrine and the series of artificial lakes he built there remain.

Ancient Temple
The Confucius Temple in Beijing was built under Mongol rule in 1306.

to ensure that the most talented people served in the government, no matter who was ruling. The civil service exam mainly tested one's knowledge of the ideas of Confucius (c. 551–479 B.C.E.), one of China's greatest thinkers. The Great Khan, however, did not trust the followers of Confucius who dominated Chinese politics. He was more interested in selecting civil servants who were loyal to him. Khubilai turned to foreigners for many upper positions, although Chinese held lower positions in the government.

Other East Asian Battles

Even before he had complete control of China, Khubilai looked to further conquests in East Asia. His first concern was Korea, which Chinggis had invaded in 1218. The first Great Khan forced the Koreans to pay tribute to him, but they stopped making this payment a few years later. The Mongols invaded Korea again in 1231, but the country did not come under firm Mongol control until the end of Möngke's reign, in 1258. Khubilai formed good relations with Wonjong (r. 1259–1274), the Korean king who ruled with the Mongols' permission, so when several Korean military leaders rebelled, Khubilai sent troops to aid the king.

In 1273, as the war with the Song went on, Khubilai ordered some of his forces to Japan. For years, he had been sending ambassadors there, demanding that the Japanese pay him tribute as both the emperor of China and the Great Khan of the Mongols. The Japanese, however, always refused his demands.

In 1274 a Mongol fleet of about 800 boats sailed for Japan, carrying an invasion force of more than 30,000 Mongol, Chinese, and Korean soldiers and sailors. In the first battle on the island of Kyushu the Mongols scored a decisive victory, but a severe storm forced their soldiers to return to their ships. The vessels sailed into opens seas to escape damage from the fierce winds, but the plan backfired. The storm battered the ships at sea, resulting in heavy Mongol losses. The surviving forces returned to China.

Khubilai was not ready to forget the Japanese, and he sent an even larger army to Japan in 1281. This time, the Japanese fought well and another damaging storm forced the Mongol forces to retreat. Japan never faced another Mongol threat.

Khubilai and his forces were more successful in Southeast Asia. In 1277, Mongol forces invaded the kingdom of Pagan, in what is now Myanmar (Burma). The Burmese rode elephants into battle, and the Mongol general ordered his archers to shoot at the animals, not the riders. Marco Polo described the scene in *The Description of the World*, writing that the elephants "were wounded on every side of the body . . . and were frightened by the great noise of the shouting." The frenzied animals ran toward the Burmese troops, "putting the army of the king . . . into the greatest confusion." The Mongol victory led to only limited control over Pagan, and Khubilai sent more troops there during the 1280s, forcing the kingdom to pay tribute.

Mongol influence also reached into what is now Vietnam and part of Indonesia. The Mongol army fought a series of battles with two Vietnamese kingdoms, Annam and Champa, and invaded the Indonesian island of Java in 1292. For a time, the kings of the two Vietnamese kingdoms paid tribute, but Khubilai never had direct control over their lands. The invasion of Java, like the earlier attacks on Japan, ended in failure.

Conflicts in the West

Khubilai focused most of his attention and military might on East Asia, but he did not overlook the western part of his empire. He had no choice, as rebellion and outside threats threatened his rule. The region of Tibet, which includes modern Tibet and parts of Qinghai and Sichuan Provinces in China, had been under Mongol influence since the late 1240s. During the 1280s, a group of Tibetans rebelled against the leader Khubilai had chosen for the region. The Great Khan sent in soldiers, who killed about 10,000 Tibetans while squashing the rebellion.

One of Khubilai's concerns about the Tibetan rebels was their tie to an old enemy, his cousin Khaidu (1236–1301), a grandson of the Great Khan Ögedei. Khaidu was based in the region around Lake Balkhash, east of Transoxiana, in part of the Chaghatai Khanate. Khaidu eventually made a deal with the Mongols of the Golden Horde and Barak (d. 1271), a great-grandson of Chaghatai who ruled the family's *ulus*. The arrangement gave

FISH FIT FOR A KING
As part of their tribute to Khubilai Khan, the Koreans sent fish. The Great Khan did not eat them—he used their skin to make his shoes. (Most Mongols wore shoes made of pressed felt.) The Mongols believed animal skins and organs could have curative properties, especially if they were fresh.

Khaidu control of large parts of the Chaghatai *ulus*. Eventually, Khaidu was powerful enough to choose the khan who ruled that *ulus*, though he had the supreme authority. With his growing power, Khaidu repeatedly challenged Khubilai in the western part of his khanate.

For several years, Khaidu let Chaghatai princes under his control do most of the fighting. These Central Asian Mongols fought skirmishes against troops led by Nomukhan (d. c. 1292), Khubilai's son. In 1276 some of the commanders under Nomukhan plotted against him. They kidnapped the Mongol prince, his brother, and cousin, bringing Nomukhan and his brother to the khan of the Golden Horde and the third captive to Khaidu. Although he welcomed the action, Khaidu did not take an active part in the plot. The kidnapping added to Khubilai's troubles in the region; rebels in Mongolia then perceived him as being weak in that part of his realm. In 1277, the rebels looted Karakorum, the old Mongol capital, and Khubilai had to send troops to end the rebellion. Some of the escaping rebels later joined forces with Khaidu.

The major conflict between Khaidu and Khubilai began in 1286. Khaidu seized the city of Besh-baliq, south of the Altai Mountains. The next year, a Mongol prince named Nayan (d. 1287) led a rebellion in Manchuria, a region in northern China. He and Khaidu were working together, and Khaidu took advantage of the revolt to invade western Mongolia. Khubilai personally led the campaign against Nayan, which ended with the rebel's capture and execution. Marco Polo observed the battle and wrote in *The Travels of Marco Polo* that "from this and from that such cries arose from the crowds of the wounded and the dying that had God thundered, you would not have heard Him!"

Nayan's death did not end Khaidu's efforts against Khubilai. Khaidu continued advancing into Mongolia for several years, until his death in 1301. By that time, Khubilai was already dead and the title of Great Khan had passed on to his grandson, Temür Öljeitü. For a time under his rule, the conflicts between the various khanates ended, and Mongol China began a peaceful period that lasted several decades.

The Development of the Ilkhanate

Until the 1250s, Mongol control in eastern Persia and surrounding lands was not complete, because some local rulers still held power. Although Chinggis had won important victories in Khorazm and Khurasan, a region in Iran, it took Hülegü's campaign in 1256 to truly bring the region into the empire. Hülegü was the first khan of what was eventually called the

Ilkhanate. *Il* is a Mongol word meaning "controlled" or "not rebellious." The name reflected the fact that Hülegü accepted Khubilai as the Great Khan and would not challenge his authority.

Hülegü's khanate stretched from the Oxus River and the Hindu Kush to Anatolia, which is now the major part of modern Turkey. The Ilkhanate's southern border was the Persian Gulf and the Arabian Sea. On the north was the *ulus* of the Golden Horde. Some of the modern nations within the Ilkhanate's borders are Armenia, Georgia, Azerbaijan, Iran, Iraq, and parts of Afghanistan, Pakistan, and Turkmenistan. As khan, Hülegü showed far more restraint than he had during his earlier conquest of Baghdad. After Hülegü died, the Christian historian Bar Hebraeus wrote (as quoted by David Nicholle in *The Mongol Warlords*), "The wisdom of this man, and his greatness of soul, and his wonderful actions are incomparable."

Seeking a Western Alliance

In 1262, Hülegü tried to make contact with leaders in Western Europe, looking for allies against the Mamluks and the Golden Horde. A letter that he wrote to King Louis IX of France survives, and Hülegü also sent diplomats to Italy. Abagha (d. 1282), Hülegü's son and the second Ilkhan, continued these efforts to find allies in the West. Letters from him reached Pope Urban IV, the head of the Roman Catholic Church, and King Edward I of England. Abagha also signed a trade treaty with Venice, whose merchants sold goods at trading posts along the Black Sea. Politically, however, the Mongol effort to win Western allies failed. No European leaders sent troops to help Abagha fight the Mamluks.

While ruling the Ilkhanate, Hülegü faced problems on several sides. One of his enemies was his cousin Berke, third khan of the Golden Horde. Berke did not support Khubilai's election as the Great Khan, which placed him and Hülegü on opposite sides of the Chinggisid family. The two cousins also had a border dispute, battling over Azerbaijan. Finally, Berke converted to Islam, and he disliked Hülegü's leniency toward Christians and other people who did not practice Islam. Berke joined the Mamluks of Egypt in an alliance against the Ilkhanate.

In 1262, Berke and the Mamluks launched attacks on Hülegü from two fronts. The Mamluk leader Baybars (1233–1277) fought Christians in Syria and Armenia who were allied with Hülegü. Berke's forces invaded Hülegü's lands in Georgia and Azerbaijan, and the two sides also fought in southern Russia. In 1263, the Golden Horde won a major victory at the Terek River. Retreating forces from the Ilkhanate drowned when the ice on the river gave way. The loss, however, spurred Hülegü to launch a major offensive the following year. A rebellion in his empire delayed the attack, though, and Hülegü died in 1265 before he could lead the army against his cousin. Hülegü's son Abagha then took command, and two major Mongol armies prepared to go to war. The war, however, never fully developed. Berke died in 1266, and the next khan of the Golden Horde, Möngke Temür (d. 1280), decided not to continue the struggle with the Ilkhanate.

Soon after one struggle with a relative ended, Abagha faced a new threat from another. Barak, from the Chaghatai *ulus*, attacked the eastern borders of the Ilkhanate. In 1269, he took over part of Khurasan. Abagha eventually pushed the invaders out of his realm and carried the counterattack into Transoxiana.

Around the same time, Baybars attacked Antioch in Syria and invaded Armenia. In 1277 he fought Mongol forces in Anatolia and Lesser Armenia, a Christian kingdom allied with the Ilkhanate. (Today this area is part of Turkey.) Abagha launched a successful counterattack, but the

The Gates of Baghdad
A 13th-century manuscript shows the Mongols storming Baghdad in 1288. Under Arghun, the Mongols of the Ilkhanate rejected Islam.

Mamluks continued to threaten the western edges of his lands. In 1281 Abagha led a major invasion of Syria. He hoped to do what his father had not: defeat the Mamluks and extend Mongol rule as far west as Egypt. Once again, however, the Mamluks repelled the Mongols.

Unrest in the Ilkhanate

Abagha died after the failed invasion of Syria, and in 1282 his brother Teguder (d. 1284) emerged as the next Ilkhan. He prevented Abagha's son Arghun (c. 1258–1291) from taking over as Abagha

CONNECTIONS >>>>>>>>>>>>

The Ilkhan's Capital

Abagha set up his capital at Tabriz, a city in what is now northwest Iran. Abagha relied on Persian officials to run his government from there, and it served as the capital of the Ilkhanate until Sultaniyya was built early in the 14th century. Tabriz was a center of art and commerce as well the capital. Remains of a Mongol fortress still stand in the city, which is one of the largest in modern Iran. However, the Mongol rulers continued to lead a nomadic life, and capitals were more for the locals than the Mongols.

had wanted. Teguder, a convert to Islam, then tried to forge an alliance with the Muslims of Egypt. But before he could make the Ilkhanate an Islamic state, however, Teguder was assassinated by Arghun and Mongol princes loyal to him. Historian Paul D. Buell, in his *Historical Dictionary of the Mongol World Empire*, writes that Arghun's rule "began with a bloodbath," as the new Ilkhan and his supporters killed the officials who had supported Teguder.

For most of Arghun's reign, his empire was at peace. But like his father and grandfather before him, he was determined to capture Syria and destroy the Mamluks. And like them, he reached out to the West, hoping to unite Mongol and Christian armies against the Muslims. He wrote letters and sent diplomats, and at one point promised to provide 30,000 horses for Christian soldiers to use in Syria. In a letter to Pope Honorius IV (c. 1201–1287), the head of the Roman Catholic Church, the Ilkhan wrote (as quoted by J. A. Boyle in *The Cambridge History of Iran*), "[W]e from this side and you from your side shall crush [Egypt] between us with good men." Although a wartime alliance never developed, Arghun did strengthen his business ties with West. In 1288, he signed a contract with merchants from Genoa, Italy, similar to the one his father had signed with Venice.

With Arghun's death in 1291, the Ilkhanate entered an unstable period. The Ilkhan had not named his successor, so the next year his brother Geikhatu (c. 1271–1295) took power. He spent money lavishly and soon ran into financial trouble. Within four years, rebels led by Baidu

(d. 1295), a grandson of Hülegü, strangled Geikhatu. Baidu then claimed the title of Ilkhan. Almost immediately, Arghun's son Ghazan (1271–1304) challenged Baidu's authority. Although once a Buddhist, Ghazan followed the advice of one of his generals and converted to Islam. This made him popular with many of the local people. By the end of 1295, Ghazan had won enough support to force out Baidu and become the next Ilkhan.

A Welcome Reign

Under Ghazan, the Ilkhanate reached its cultural and economic peak. J.A. Boyle, in *The Cambridge History of Iran*, calls him "without question the greatest of the Il-Khans, a remarkably gifted man by the standards of any age." Ghazan promoted the arts and education, and constructed many grand public buildings. He also continued reforms begun under Arghun to create a centralized tax system. Historians are not sure how many of these reforms actually took place, but at least on paper he was doing his best to improve the government.

Through his actions, Ghazan sometimes showed two sides. He tried to make life easier and fairer for the common people, and he ordered Mongol officials to stop beating and killing the peasants' wives and children. The Mongols sometimes used these violent tactics to convince the local people to pay their taxes. Yet at times Ghazan could be ruthless as he enforced the laws of his land. Official records show that in just one month, he executed 43 high-ranking officials, including Mongol princes.

During Ghazan's reign, more Mongols began to convert to Islam. Ghazan's reign began with a wave of persecution against Christians and Buddhists, but he later stopped these forced conversions. Some Mongols also gave up their nomadic lifestyle and began marrying local peoples, especially the Turks. Their distinct Mongol culture began to blend with the native Turkic and Persian cultures. This process continued for decades. Ghazan, however, always remained proud of his Mongol heritage and his family ties to Chinggis Khan. He studied the history of his family and their rule, and he continued to respect the authority of Temür, Khubilai Khan's successor in China.

Following Mongol tradition, Ghazan looked beyond his borders for lands to conquer. First on the list was Mamluk Syria, and the Ilkhanate managed to seize the city of Aleppo in 1299. A second invasion in 1303 ended horribly for the Mongols. After their defeat, Mongol prisoners were forced to march through Cairo. Around their necks they carried the heads of other Mongols which the Mamluks had chopped off. Ghazan died

CHINESE ADVENTURER

One of the diplomats Arghun sent to the West was Rabban Sauma (c. 1230–1293), a Christian priest from China who was an ethnic Turk. Khubilai Khan had sent Sauma to the Ilkhanate as his official representative. Arghun then sent him to Europe, hoping he could win support from Christian leaders for his attack on Syria. Sauma traveled in reverse almost the same route Marco Polo took on his trip to Khubilai's court. Sauma was the first Chinese traveler to reach Paris and other cities of Western Europe, visiting them between 1275 and 1280.

the following year, with the Mongol dream of spreading their empire to Egypt still unfulfilled. The end of his rule also marked the end of a strong Mongol presence in the Ilkhanate. The realm would take on greater Persian and Muslim influence in the years to come.

The Golden Horde

Of the three khanates beyond the Mongols' homeland in East Asia, the Golden Horde had the least contact with the Great Khan. They were the farthest away, and Möngke and Khubilai were more focused on China than other parts of the realm. The Kipchak Khanate, as the Mongols called it, had fewer Mongols than the other *ulus*. It also had fewer officials who reported to the Great Khan, giving the local khans greater independence.

The Golden Horde's capital was Saray, along the Volga River and not far from the Caspian Sea. The Mongols had direct control over most of the region near the Volga, the southern steppes of Russia, and lands north of the Caucasus Mountains, which run between the Black and Caspian Seas. The ulus also spread into parts of Siberia and what is now Khazakstan. The khans of the Golden Horde also had indirect control over northwest Russia and other parts of Eastern Europe. The first Kipchak khan, Batu, used his power to convince some Russian princes to surrender without a fight. He sent Prince Alexander Nevsky (1220–1263) this message (as quoted by John Lawrence in *A History of Russia*): "God has subdued many nations to me; dost thou alone refuse to submit to my power? But if thou wishest to keep thy lands, come to me. . . . " To keep their local authority, Nevsky and the other Russian princes paid the Mongols tribute.

As noted earlier, some of the Golden Horde's conflicts with the rest of the empire arose over the selection of new Great Khans. Batu accepted Möngke as the Great Khan, but his brother Berke refused to back Khubilai's election in 1260. Berke also feuded

The Best for the Horses
This gilded silver ornament was part of the tack for a horse. It was made in the area around the Black Sea in Russia, in the 13th or 14th century.

with the Ilkhanate, his neighbor to the southwest. Berke and his successors' wars with the Ilkhans led them to become allies of the Mamluks of Egypt, the major enemy of the Ilkhanate. That friendship made the Golden Horde and the Mamluks trading partners as well as military allies. Contact with the Turkic rulers of Egypt also strengthened Turkic culture among the elite in the Kipchak khanate. The Mongols in Russia did not absorb local culture, as the Mongols did in Persia and China. They chose to isolate themselves on the steppes and follow the traditional nomadic culture as much as possible.

The Rise of Noghai

Starting in the 1260s, a Mongol prince named Noghai (d. 1299) gained considerable power within the Golden Horde. He was the nephew of Berke, and in 1259 he led a Mongol army into Poland. The advance was a brief detour from a campaign against rebels on the western edge of the khanate. Six years later, Noghai led a larger force into Bulgaria. Berke was responding to a plea for help from the Bulgarians, who faced an invasion from the Byzantine Empire, which was based in Constantinople (modern Istanbul) in what is now Turkey. The Byzantine Empire had once been a major force in Eastern Europe and parts of the Middle East, although its power was declining by this time. The Mongols of Russia sometimes came into conflict with the Byzantine Empire, as they competed with it for influence over smaller countries in the region. Given this strained relationship, the Mongols agreed to help the Bulgarians.

Noghai forced the Byzantine troops out of Bulgaria, and he eventually married a member of the Byzantine royal family—a sign that the Byzantines wanted an alliance with the Mongols rather than continued fighting. Noghai eventually became a so-called kingmaker: He never ruled as khan of the Golden Horde, but he chose who held that title and influenced key government decisions.

In 1265, Noghai and Berke launched an attack on Ilkhanate territory, hoping to win control of Azerbaijan and Georgia. During one battle in 1266, the khan was killed and Noghai lost an eye. The new khan was Möngke Temür, who was either the son or grandson of Batu (the records are not clear). The new leader of the Golden Horde ended the war with the Ilkhanate. He also continued to assert the Golden Horde's independence from Khubilai Khan, supporting the Great Khan's foe, Khaidu, in Central Asia. In another small but symbolic move, Möngke Temür removed any mention of Khubilai from his kingdom's coins.

ALEXANDER NEVSKY

Alexander Nevsky, who controlled the northern Russian city of Novgorod, worked with the Mongols because he thought his true enemies were Westerners—Germans, Lithuanians, and Swedes. Nevsky also seems to have helped himself and his family financially through his relations with the Mongols. When the Soviet Union was fighting Germany during World War II, Russians saw Nevsky as a national hero. The film *Alexander Nevksy*, about his battles with the Germans, is considered a classic and is still shown today.

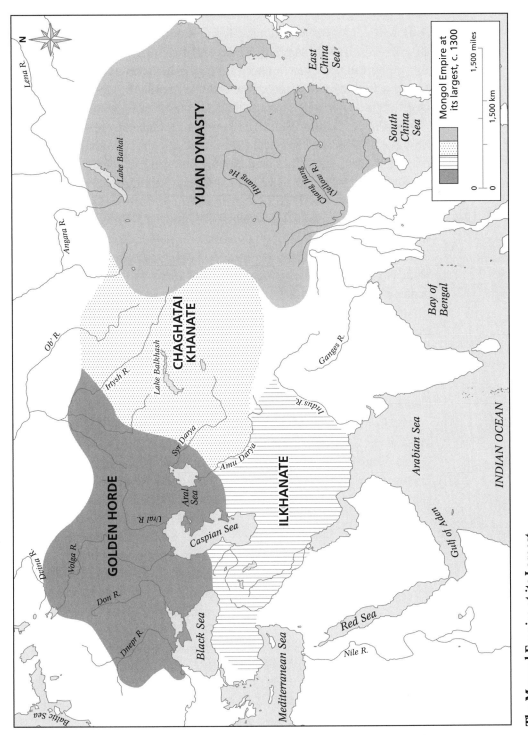

The Mongol Empire at its Largest

The Mongol Empire, c. 1300, was divided into four mini-empires, each ruled by a descendant of Chinggis Khan.

Return to Europe

Although not a Muslim, Möngke Temür maintained the Golden Horde's strong relations with Mamluk Egypt. He also sought good terms with the Byzantine Empire, since it controlled the sea routes that linked Mongol Russia with the Middle East. Under Möngke Temür, the Golden Horde was largely at peace, and it continued to collect taxes from its Russian subjects.

Möngke Temür died in 1280 and was replaced by his brother Tode Möngke (d. 1287). After he converted to Islam, the new khan focused on religion more than politics, and Noghai practically ruled the khanate for him. Noghai controlled a part of the khanate that bordered the Black Sea and Eastern Europe. In 1285, Noghai led Mongol forces into Europe, at the request of the Hungarian king Ladislas IV (1262–1290), a semi-pagan who was battling Hungary's Christian barons for power.

During this invasion of Europe, Noghai occupied Transylvania in what is now Romania. Another Mongol force, led by Tode Möngke's nephew Telebogha (d. 1291), tried to enter Hungary through the Carpathian Mountains. Snow stopped the Mongols' movement, so the frustrated troops then sacked the nearby towns. In 1286, Noghai and the second Mongol force combined for an invasion of Poland, but this time the Poles held off the Mongols. After this largely unsuccessful campaign, the Mongols never again attacked Poland or Hungary. Noghai, however, continued to have influence in Bulgaria and other parts of southeastern Europe.

After returning from battle, Telebogha soon took over as the next khan of the Golden Horde. He and Noghai competed for power within Russia. When a group of Mongol princes wanted to replace Telebogha with his son Tokto'a (d. 1312), Noghai joined the plot to kill the khan, and beginning in 1291, he acted as the khan of the Golden Horde, although he did not hold the title.

Tokto'a, however, was eager to assert his rule, as he and Noghai quarreled over how the Golden Horde should conduct its trade and diplomacy. The Italian city of Genoa dominated trade in the Crimean, a peninsula on the Black Sea. Genoese merchants there asked Tokto'a to protect them from Noghai, who was trying to end their control of the Crimean trade. Tok-

CONNECTIONS >>>>>>>>>>>>

Royal Title

The Russians gave all the khans of the Golden Horde the title of *tsar* or *czar*, which means "caesar," a reference to Julius Caesar and the later Roman emperors of Byzantium. Later Russian rulers, who copied many Mongol methods of governing, also used this title.

to'a went to war with the Mongol tsar, and his forces killed Noghai in 1299.

By this time problems were developing in Russia. Mongol tax collectors, known as *basqaqs*, faced the threat of violence from local residents as they carried out their duties. Tokto'a had to rely more and more heavily on the local princes to collect taxes, which gave them more influence. He traveled north from Saray to meet with them, making him the first khan since Batu to leave the steppe and enter the forests of Russia. Tokto'a never completed his journey, however; he died along the way.

Tokto'a's nephew Ozbek (d. 1341) became the next khan of the Golden Horde. In Russia, he made a major political move in 1327 when he named Ivan I (d. 1341;

Noghai and Ozbek's People

Noghai's lands near the Carpathians were sometimes called the Noghai Horde, and the tribes there were later known as the Noghai. The people included various Turkic ethnic groups. Descendants of these former citizens of the Mongol Empire are still called the Noghai. Some live in a region of Russia called Daghestan, north of the Caucasus Mountains. Other Noghai live in parts of Romania.

In some sources, Ozbek's name is written as Uzbek. That name was carried into Central Asia when invaders from part of the old Golden Horde crossed into Transoxiana. These invaders were called Uzbeks, and their name is at the root of the name Uzbekistan, a region of what was once the Soviet Union. In 1991, Uzbekistan declared its independence.

also called Ivan Kalita) of Moscow the Grand Prince of Russia. Ivan had helped the Mongols end a revolt in the city of Tver, north of Moscow. After this, the political and economic power among the Russians shifted to Moscow. The Russians, however, were still not strong enough to challenge Mongol rule.

Under Ozbek, Islam became the official religion of the khanate, yet he also tried to keep good relations with Christian lands. He still battled with the Ilkhanate, trying to gain land at his Mongol cousins' expense, but like the Golden Horde rulers before him, he failed. By the 1320s the Mamluks and the Ilkhanate had made peace, so the Egyptian Turks had even less reason to help Ozbek. Although the Golden Horde had not lost territory, its power had reached its peak and other peoples in the region were growing stronger. Throughout the empire once ruled by the Great Khans, the period of military conquest was largely over. Over the next decades, outside threats and internal changes weakened the Mongols' rule in all the khanates.

CHAPTER 3

Final Years of the Khanates

THE EARLY YEARS OF THE 14TH CENTURY MARKED THE PEAK of Mongol influence across Eurasia. Throughout that century, the four khanates went through many changes, and by 1400 the Mongols' presence in the lands they had conquered varied widely. In some places, Mongol influence had almost disappeared. In others, it took on new forms or passed on to rulers with few or no direct ties to the great Chinggis Khan.

China After Khubilai Khan

With the death of Khubilai Khan in 1294, Mongol rule in China passed to his grandson Tëmur Öljeitü (d. 1307). He largely carried out Khubilai's policies, though he ended plans for another attack on Japan and Vietnam. The Chinese Mongol emperors ruled only China and the Mongol homeland.

Tëmur Öljeitü had several successors in just a short period. They faced a familiar problem: balancing the interests of Mongol princes who favored traditional Mongolian customs with the interests of the pro-Chinese Mongols and the Chinese themselves. One positive change came for the Chinese who followed the ideas of Confucius. The emperor Ayurbarwada (d. 1320) brought back the old civil service exam system (see page 34). Of all the Mongol rulers of the Yuan Dynasty, he was one of the most comfortable with Chinese culture, and was able to speak and read Chinese.

A period of turmoil began in 1322, when Shidebala (d. 1322), Ayurbarwada's son, was assassinated. Various members of the Mongol royal family and their Chinese supporters competed for power, erupting in 10 years of civil war. Finally, in 1333, the last Mongol ruler in China emerged. Toghan Temür (d. 1368) was 13 years old when he took the throne. He reigned for 35 years–the longest since Khubilai–but faced many problems.

OPPOSITE
The Last Great Khan
Tamerlane, the last of the great Mongol rulers, inspired fear and awe among Europeans for centuries after his death. This is an Italian engraving from 1600.

China was hit with serious floods and epidemics during Toghan Temür's reign. But some of his problems stemmed from Mongol rule and the Chinese reaction to it. Many people of southern China had never truly accepted the Mongols. They also resented the growing power of the local officials who taxed them and basically ran their lives. In 1325, peasants in the south revolted, and by the 1340s groups of armed bandits were taking control of southern towns, sometimes working with local governments. The power of the central government in the south weakened, leading to the growth of regional governments with their own informal armies. Going into the 1350s, the emperor and his supporters controlled the region around Khan-baliq, but not much else.

Toghan Temür and his generals had trouble resisting the growing threat to their rule. They could not recruit troops from the Mongol homeland because its population had fallen during the 14th century due to earlier wars and the need for Mongol soldiers in other parts of the empire. Toghan Temür added to his problems by relying on warlords to defend his empire; these generals were more concerned with winning power at one another's expense than they were with maintaining the empire.

The rebels also sometimes fought among themselves, slowing their efforts to drive out the Mongols. By 1356, however, a Chinese peasant soldier named Zhu Yuanzhang (1328–1398) emerged as the leader of a unified rebel army. As a boy, Zhu studied Buddhism and learned to read and write, giving him more education than the average peasant. He first led a small band of rebels, then defeated competing rebel bands to gain power. He eventually became the founder of the next Chinese dynasty, the Ming. Zhu established his own government in Nanjing, in southeastern China, then slowly moved his forces northward. During this time, the Mongol warlords continued to fight with one another, which kept them from launching an effective counterattack in the south.

In 1368, as Zhu's armies neared Khan-baliq, Toghan Temür escaped north to Shangdu before fleeing toward Mongolia. Legend says six *tümens*—60,000 Mongols—joined him, but this is difficult to confirm. Others stayed in China for several more years, trying to hold off the rebels, but the Chinese regained complete control of their country by 1382. Some Mongols remained in China and were absorbed into the population.

Although defeated, Toghan Temür did not give up his claim to be the emperor of China. After his death in 1370, his son and grandson tried to reassert Mongol authority from a base in northern China. The Chinese, however, forced the Mongols to retreat to their homeland. Another battle

THE INFLUENCE OF THE LAMAS

Ayurbarwada and Shidebala were given the titles Buyantu ("meritorius") and Gegen ("shining"), respectively, in Mongolian. They also had Chinese names when they came to power: Ayurbarwada was called Renzong and his son was known as Yingzong. Today they are often called by the Sanskrit names used here. Sanskrit was one of the first languages used to write down Buddhist texts. The Mongols' use of Sanskrit names shows the influence of the Tibetan lamas at the Yuan royal court.

in 1387 led to a devastating Mongol defeat, and the Chinese eventually destroyed the old Mongol capital of Karakorum.

In 1399, the last of Khubilai's descendants to claim the authority to rule China was assassinated. Other Mongol leaders began competing for power in and around Mongolia. In the west of Mongolia, a group of Mongols called the Oirat began to develop a mini-empire. Mongols who still claimed family ties to Chinggis rose to power in the east. As the two groups struggled for power, the Chinese tried to take advantage, launching an attack in the early 1400s. The Chinese won a major battle in 1410, but within 15 years the eastern Mongols were raiding China, which led to a huge Chinese counterattack on Mongolia. The invasion did not destroy the eastern Mongols, however.

With the eastern Mongols weakened, the Oirat tried to build a united Mongol state. Their relations with China wavered; at times the Ming emperors seemed friendly, but ultimately the Chinese did not want a strong Mongol presence on their border. In 1439, the Oirat leader Esen (d. 1455) came to power. He married into Chinggis's family to claim some ties to the former Great Khan, then gained control over the other Mongol tribes. In 1449, Esen led an invasion of China and his troops captured the Ming emperor Zhu Zhizhen (r. 1436–1449). The modern historians Woodbridge Bingham, Hilary Conroy, and Fred Ilké, in *A History of Asia*, say the captured emperor "sat serenely, showing no emotions whatsoever among 100,000 Chinese corpses and his slaughtered bodyguard." The Ming decided not to try to get their kidnapped emperor back. Instead, they named a new emperor and continued to fight the Mongols.

But Esen's war in China stirred up trouble within his own empire, as the eastern Mongolians preferred not to fight the Chinese, fearing the costs were too high for too unlikely a prize. Esen's assassination in 1455 sparked a civil war. Finally, an eastern Mongol named Dayan Khan (d. c. 1517), a descendant of the family of Khubilai Khan, came to power around 1480. Under

CONNECTIONS >>>>>>>>>>>

More Bricks in the Wall

Ming Dynasty emperors began rebuilding the Great Wall, an unconnected series of low defensive earthworks running across northern China, in 1470. New sections were added, old sections were fortified, and isolated sections were connected. They hoped the rebuilt and strengthened wall would hold back the Mongols and other raiders from the steppes. The Great Wall that still exists in China dates from this period. Today the Great Wall stretches for more than 4,200 miles as it zigzags across northern China.

CONNECTIONS >>>>>>>>>>>>

Two "Universal" Leaders

The Mongol title *dalai* was first given to a Tibetan lama by Altan Khan. *Dalai* is a Mongolian word meaning "vast sea" or "great ocean." It is similar to Chinggis's title, which means "oceanic" (universal), so the Dalai Lama was also considered a "universal" leader. The Tibetans believe that each Dalai Lama is the reincarnation of the first one proclaimed by the Mongol khan. Today, the head of Tibetan Buddhism is the 14th Dalai Lama. Reflecting the close cultural link between the Mongols and the Tibetans, Tibetan Buddhism (sometimes called Lamaism) is still the major religion in Mongolia.

The 14th Dalai Lama is the head of Tibetan Buddhism.

him and his grandson Altan Khan (1507–1583), the eastern Mongols took back much of the traditional Mongol homeland from China. More important for future developments in Mongolia, Altan Khan made Tibetan Buddhism the nation's official religion.

Struggles in Persia

In the Ilkhanate, the peak of Mongol rule came under Ghazan. With his death in 1304, the Ilkhanate entered an unstable period. Princes in the royal family fought for control. Ghazan had picked his brother Kharbanda (c. 1280–1316) as his successor, and Kharbanda killed several relatives he considered rivals. He then took power under the name Öljeitü, which means "fortunate."

Around this time, the four branches of the Mongol empire entered a brief period of cooperation. As Öljeitü noted in a letter to the king of France (cited by J.A. Boyle in *The Cambridge History of Iran*), ". . . protected by Heaven, all of us, elder and younger brothers, reached a mutual agreement. . . ." This relationship, however, did not mean the Great Khan was once again ruling over a united empire. In practice, the four khanates continued to go their separate ways, grapple with their own problems, and sometimes compete for land and power.

Öljeitü, like his brother, hoped to continue fighting the

Mamluks of Egypt. He also hoped to receive help from the Christian rulers of Europe. But his more immediate problem was in Gilan, an area near the Caspian Sea. During fierce fighting there, the Mongols won several battles before the local residents managed a major victory. Eventually, Gilan was conquered, but at a very high cost. By 1308, Öljeitü learned that the European kings were not eager to help him battle the Mamluks. In 1312, he launched his only attack against the Ilkhanate's long-time enemy. A month-long siege in the Mamluks' Syrian lands failed, and Öljeitü retreated. The Mongols would never again invade Mamluk territory.

The Crumbling Ilkhanate

Two major decisions during Öljeitü's rule affected life within the khanate: Öljeitü converted to the Shiite branch of Islam, and he appointed Rashid al-Din to run the southern half of the realm and Ali Shah (d. 1324) to run the north. (This system of splitting the daily operations of the government between two advisors existed through all the Ilkhans). Both decisions led to problems. Sunni Muslims in the realm disliked the Shiites and the official recognition that came with such a prominent conversion. This led to conflict between the two factions within the government. And the two advisors' battle for control eventually led Ali Shah's allies to accuse Rashid al-Din of poisoning Öljeitü, who died in 1316. The charge was false, but that did not stop Mongol officials from executing the great scholar and government official by cutting his body in half.

After Rashid's death, a general named Choban (d. 1327) served as the chief advisor to the new Ilkhan, Abu Said (c. 1304–1335), who was Öljeitü's son. Abu Said came to power when he was only 12. Around 1320 Abu Said and Choban led a military force that fought off an attack in Azerbaijan from the Mongols of the Golden Horde. Another Mongol, a Chaghatai prince, led a rebellion in 1319 in Khorasan, in what is now northeast Iran. The Ilkhanate was also able to end this threat.

Abu Said ruled well over the Ilkhanate until his death. He signed a peace treaty with the Mamluks, and he kept the government together as different groups within it competed for power. With his death, however, Ilkhanate politics became chaotic. Abu Said did not have a son nor any male relative to take his place; he was the last descendant of the great Mongol conqueror Hülegü to rule. Mongol princes with distant ties to Chinggis began fighting for control. These civil wars gave other ethnic groups—Persians, Arabs, Turks—a chance to drive the Mongols out of power. Most historians cite 1353 as the end of the Ilkhanate.

MAN OF MANY FAITHS

Öljeitü provides an example of the influence different religions had across the Mongol Empire. He was baptized a Christian as a child, but later in life he converted to Buddhism and then Sunni Islam, before ending up a Shiite.

Conflict and Change in the Golden Horde

The peak of the Golden Horde's power in Russia came at the beginning of the 14th century. This period of relative peace and prosperity ended after the reign of Ozbek, who died in 1341. The Golden Horde had a series of khans after this. As different leaders competed for power, sometimes troops fought one another. The Golden Horde also faced a threat from the east: Lithuania was becoming a military and economic power and challenging Mongol influence in the Russian cities.

During the 1370s, another challenge came from the Blue Horde in modern Kazakhstan. This Mongol group traced its roots to Orda, brother of Batu, the first khan of the Golden Horde. Mamai, an influential leader who did not belong to the Mongol royal family, supported the White Horde prince, Urus, to become khan. Urus fought for power with his nephew Toqtamish (d. 1405), who had the support of Tamerlane. Toqtamish eventually united the Golden and White Hordes under his rule.

Mamai was still involved in the khanate's politics in 1380, when the Russians made their first serious challenge to Mongol rule. Under Ozbek, Moscow had become the home of the Grand Princes of Russia, who were in charge of collecting taxes from the Russians for the Mongols. Over time, the city's rulers gained strength, compared to the other Russian leaders. In September 1380, Grand Duke Dmitri Donskoi (1350–1389) led a Muscovite army against Mamai at Kulikovo Pole, near the Don River. The Russians won a decisive victory, and Mamai's defeat guaranteed Toqtamish's rule.

In the beginning of the 1390s, Toqtamish tried to assert his independence from Tamerlane by creating an alliance with Egypt and Lithuania and acquiring new lands. Tamerlane, however, struck before Toqtamish could attack him. In 1395, Tamerlane's forces destroyed Saray, the Golden Horde's capital, and Toqtamish fled. The Golden Horde never recovered from this blow. First Tamerlane and then the Lithuanians chose their own representatives as khan. The Golden Horde gradually split into two distinct groups; neither one had much power. One center for the remaining Mongols on the steppes of southern Russia and Eastern Ukraine was Kazan, a city near the Volga River. Later, three other distinct groups of Mongols settled in Astrakhan, on the Caspian Sea, and the Crimea, near the Black Sea. In 1475, the Crimean Mongols came under the influence of the Ottomans, a Turkic people who founded an empire centered in what is now Turkey.

In 1480, Ivan III (1440–1505; called Ivan the Great), prince of Moscow, insulted the khan in Saray when he refused to kiss his stirrup. By tradition, the Russian princes had done this to show their loyalty. Histo-

THE BLACK DEATH

One problem the Golden Horde struggled with during the 1340s and 1350s was an outbreak of a highly contagious disease called bubonic plague, which was also known as the black death. During the mid-14th century, this plague spread across Asia into Europe, eventually killing millions of people. Some historians believe the black death can be traced to the Mongols, who brought it to the city of Kaffa, on the Crimean Sea. Fleas from rats and marmots, which were common in Mongolia, carried the disease. The fleas spread the disease to the Mongols, who infected the Europeans they were fighting at Kaffa. The soldiers then carried the black death home with them when they returned to Europe.

rians consider Ivan's defiance the end of Mongol rule over Moscow. Ivan went on to become one of Russia's most powerful czars.

The Great Horde, as the Mongols were now called, planned to attack Moscow to punish Ivan, but they retreated before reaching the city. The Saray khan feared a war with Moscow would leave him defenseless against an attack by the Crimean Tatars. A war between the two groups of Mongols came in 1502, with the Crimean branch destroying the Great Horde. Moscow was now the dominant power in what had once been the heart of the Golden Horde, and it would go on to create the modern state of Russia. In 1552, the Russians took control of Kazan and Astrakhan, ending the Mongol presence there, and the remaining Mongols in the Crimea posed only a minor threat to Russian power.

Split in the Ulus Chaghatai

In the decades after Chaghatai received his *ulus* from Chinggis, the Mongols of Central Asia remained nomadic. The first khan there to turn to a sedentary lifestyle was Kebeg (d. 1326), who built a palace in Transoxiana.

Blessing Before Battle
Saint Sergius blesses Grand Duke Dmitri Donskoi and his army on their way to the Battle of Kulikovo Pole in this Russian frieze.

53

His brother Tarmashirin (d. 1334) followed him to the throne. Tarmashirin converted to Islam and tried to extend Mongol rule into the borderlands separating his khanate and India. At times the Mongols raided India itself, but they did not control territory there. The khanate's borders, however, were larger than they had originally been because the Chaghatai rulers had earlier gained control over land in Afghanistan and the eastern edges of Persia.

Tarmashirin's conversion to Islam angered Mongols of the Ulus Chaghatai, who were loyal to the old nomadic culture. These conservative Mongols were based in the eastern part of the khanate, in southeastern Kazakhstan, Kyrgyzstan, and Xinjiang. Their territory was sometimes called Moghulistan, or "land of the Mongols." The conservatives forced Tarmashirin from power in 1334. The khans who followed him returned to the old Mongol religion. In the western half of the khanate, Turkic Muslim princes gained influence and they began to choose descendants of Chaghatai and Ögedei as khans, while the princes held the real power. This region, centered in Transoxiana, was still called the Ulus Chaghatai.

The eastern and western halves of the khanate began to drift apart. The western half was largely sedentary, Turkic, and Muslim. Moghulistan also had a Turkic and Muslim influence, but was more nomadic and stayed closer to the Mongols' cultural roots. Around 1347, however, Islam became the official religion there with the rise of the Muslim leader Tughluq Temür (d. 1363). He claimed to have family ties to Chaghatai, and in 1360 he reunited the two halves of the khanate. His rule, however, was brief, as the political situation in the western half of the Ulus Chaghatai was unstable. Various tribes competed for power. Eventually, just as in the days of Temüjin before he became Chinggis Khan, one man emerged as the supreme leader and founder of a new empire: Timur-i-leng, or Tamerlane.

The Rise of Tamerlane

Born in Kish, near Samarkand, Timur was shaped by the Turko-Mongolian steppe culture that was hundreds of years old. His family had Mongol roots, and like the Mongol rulers of old, he rode horses and shot arrows from an early age. Unlike the old khans, however, he grew up in an Islamic society and spoke Turkic. Timur belonged to the Barlas tribe, an old Mongol tribe that traced its descent from one of Chaghatai's main advisors in Transoxiana. Some historians say the Barlas was the most important local tribe in the khanate, but the evidence is not clear. Timur's clan was a major one in the tribe, but not the most important, and some medieval sources say he once had to steal sheep to survive.

KULIKOVO POLE

One of the Russian chronicles supposedly records the words of a fleeing Mongol after the Russian victory at Kulikovo Pole. As quoted by Charles Halperin in *The Tatar Yoke*, the Mongol cried, "No longer, brethren, shall we live on our land, nor see our children . . . and no longer shall we go in battle against the Rus[sians], nor shall we take tribute from the Russian princes." Until recent times, Russians considered Kulikovo one of the greatest moments in their history, when they threw off the "Tatar yoke." In reality, however, Toqtamish punished the Muscovites in 1382 by destroying their city, and the Russians remained under Mongol control for another century.

As Tughluq Temür prepared to invade Transoxiana in 1360, the leader of the Barlas fled. Timur went with him, but then returned to Kish to defend the tribal lands. Some historians believe Timur saw an opportunity to take control during a time of trouble. He already had as many as 300 warriors who served under him, some from outside his tribe. Timur also had political ties with important people in Moghulistan and lands just beyond it.

When Tughluq Temür reached Kish, he chose Timur as the leader of the region. The old tribal leader returned and briefly reclaimed his position, but Timur eventually returned to power. He still had Tughluq Temür's support, and he built alliances with other tribal leaders. Soon after, Tughluq Temür clamped down on all the local leaders in Transoxiana, and for several years Timur lived in Khorasan. He and his allies returned to

Tamurid Empire
Tamerlane controlled large parts of the old Golden Horde, Ilkhanate, and Chaghtai Khanate, but he was never able to extend his reach into China.

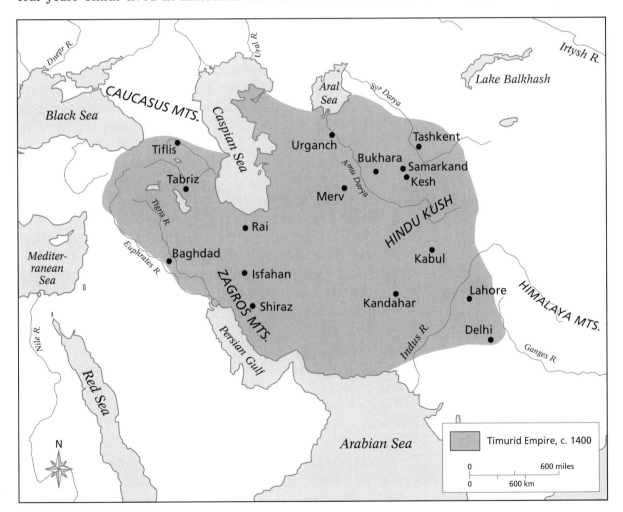

Timurid Empire, c. 1400

0   600 miles

0   600 km

Transoxiana in 1364, and in a battle that year Timur received the wounds that made him lame, leading to his nickname, "Timur the lame." That same year, his chief ally, Amir Husayn (d. 1370), took control of the Ulus Chaghatai, ending Tughluq Temür's rule there.

During the next few years Tamerlane fought a series of campaigns against forces from Moghulistan and their allies in Transoxiana. He strengthened his power by reaching out to a variety of groups: Muslims cheered his public devotion to the faith, merchants appreciated his efforts to keep trade flowing, and local princes admired his skill and leadership on the battlefield. Fighting within the Ulus Chaghatai dragged on for several years, and Tamerlane eventually fell out with with Amir Husayn, who tried to rule as a khan over Tamerlane and local princes. The two former allies eventually became the chief rivals for power in the Ulus Chaghatai.

For a time Tamerlane fought with the Moghul forces against Amir Husayn. Finally, in 1370, Tamerlane defeated his old friend and had him executed. At the same time, he claimed four of Amir Husayn's wives for himself. One of them was the daughter of a former khan of the Ulus Chaghatai. Through this wife, Tamerlane created a connection to the royal family descended from Chinggis Khan. He compared himself to the great khans and tried to win the same respect the people of Central Asia had for Chinggis and his family. But Tamerlane did not claim the title of khan. He simply referred to himself as the Great Commander and chose other men to rule as khans—while he held the real power.

Tamerlane established his capital in Samarkand and spent several years tightening his control over the Ulus Chaghatai. His troops also menaced the Moghuls and reached into Mongolia itself, though Tamerlane never had direct control over that region. In 1381, he began to attack what had once been the eastern part of the Ilkhanate, in modern-day Afghanistan. Tamerlane quickly took the city of Herat, though the citizens rebelled the next year. His forces ended the rebellion, then cut off the heads of the dead and stacked them in a pile—a practice they repeated during their conquests. Tamerlane seemed to be trying to copy Chinggis, who sometimes brutally punished enemies who resisted him. Tamerlane called himself the "scourge of God," a force sent by Heaven to punish evildoers. *The Encyclopedia of the Middle Ages* quotes Tamerlane as telling one foe, "You are wicked, but I am more wicked than you, so be silent."

From Afghanistan, Tamerlane's forces moved westward into what is now Iran. Tamerlane sought riches for himself and his army, as well as to extend his political control. And, as was the practice during the early Mon-

A RULER'S WOUNDS

In 1364 Timur was shot by several arrows in battle, causing the wounds that troubled him the rest of his life. One arrow hit his right arm, which made it impossible for him to use his right elbow. A wound in his right leg left him lame, as the leg permanently stiffened. In 1941, Russian scientists dug up Tamerlane's grave. By examining his bones they confirmed these two injuries and a third to his right hand.

gol conquests, the Great Commander would not attack cities and kingdoms if their rulers accepted his dominance.

Around 1386 Tamerlane faced a major challenge from Toqtamish, ruler of the Golden Horde. Tamerlane had helped this Mongol leader come to power, but now Toqtamish attacked the Persian city of Tabriz, which Tamerlane controlled. Tamerlane sent a huge army into Persia, and in 1387 his forces defeated the Golden Horde. During this campaign, Tamerlane's troops covered a wide area, terrorizing Georgia and parts of Anatolia. Soldiers killed some residents of Anatolia by forcing them off a cliff. Some survived because the pile of dead bodies they landed on softened their fall.

Unlike the Mongols of the 13th century, Tamerlane had trouble creating effective governments in the lands he conquered. Unrest in the defeated lands kept him from setting up strong centralized rule and forced him to return to end rebellions. In 1392, Tamerlane had to go to Iran again, beginning what is now sometimes called the Five Year Campaign. After restoring order in western Iran, the Mongol forces headed into Baghdad. David Nicolle, in *The Mongol Warlords*, quotes an anonymous historian of the time who compared Tamerlane's troops to "ants and locusts covering the whole countryside, plundering and ravaging."

From Baghdad the army headed north into Georgia and Armenia before entering the lands of the Golden Horde in 1395. Once again, Toqtamish was threatening Tamerlane's lands. Tamerlane's troops won a decisive victory, then cut off the heads, hands, and feet of civilians, destroyed Saray and Astrakhan, and chased the Golden Horde's forces back toward Moscow. With Toqtamish defeated, Tamerlane headed back to his capital in Samarkand.

His next goal was in the east, as he prepared to attack the sultanate of Delhi. This Muslim state in northern India had many Hindu residents, and Tamerlane said the sultanate's rulers should be punished for tolerating the Hindu religion. Delhi's great wealth also attracted him. In 1398, Tamerlane

CONNECTIONS >>>>>>>>>>>>

A Symbol of Evil

Tamerlane's vicious battlefield tactics spread his name throughout Eurasia. His brutality also inspired later writers to describe his life. The 16th century English playwright Christopher Marlowe (1564–1593) wrote a play about him called *Tamburlaine the Great*. American author Edgar Allen Poe's (1809–1849) first published poem was called "Tamerlane," perhaps inspired by an earlier poem by the English poet Lord Byron (1788–1824). Poe's poem deals with the emperor's lost love, not his conquests. Both poems about Tamerlane are still read today, and Marlowe's play is still sometimes performed.

and an army of about 90,000 men crossed the Indus River and destroyed the city of Delhi. Before the battle, they killed 100,000 Hindus they had taken prisoner. After it, they killed still more Hindus, as Tamerlane considered his campaign part of a holy war against the Hindus. The survivors of the massacre in Delhi later died from the famine and disease that spread through the city, and Tamerlane further reduced the population by taking many slaves.

Once again, Tamerlane was not interested in controlling territory. By March 1399, he was back in Samarkand, and within a year he was focusing on new targets in the west. After putting down another revolt in Iran, he headed toward Syria, still under the control of the Mamluks of Egypt. He took the cities of Aleppo, Hama, and Damascus. At Damascus, the capital of modern Syria, Tamerlane agreed not to destroy the city if the residents paid a tribute. They agreed and let the invaders through the city's gates, but Tamerlane then went back on his word and demanded a much larger tribute. When the Syrians refused, the warlord ordered another massacre, telling his soldiers that each should bring him the head of one resident.

Leaving Syria, the Mongol army headed north to Anatolia, as it had during the 1380s. In 1402, Tamerlane defeated an Ottoman Turk army near Ankara, the capital of modern Turkey. After collecting tribute from the cities of Anatolia, Tamerlane once again returned home.

Military and Political Life in Tamerlane's Empire

Although Tamerlane was definitely bloodthirsty and cruel, he also supported the arts and enjoyed stimulating conversations with the great thinkers of his realm. He deported artists and craftsmen from all over his conquests to Samarkand to beautify and glorify his home city. The ruler also showed practical intelligence in the way he built his army and political structures, even if he did not do as well at controlling the lands he conquered.

In creating a powerful army and recruiting political allies, Tamerlane repeated some of Chinggis's practices. The parallel was perhaps accidental, but the result was the same: Tamerlane was able to conquer large parts of Asia. Like Chinggis, he selected generals and aides for their personal loyalty, not their tribal ties. He also moved soldiers around to different regiments, so that they were not commanded by their tribal leaders. The army was organized using the same system Chinggis had used, with the *tumen* as the largest unit. Over time, Tamerlane also added conquered people to his forces, as the first Great Khan had done. The army in Tamerlane's empire eventually included pagans, Christians, and Muslims from a wide

CONNECTIONS >>>>>>>>>>>>>>>>>>>>>>>>>>>>>>>>>>>

The Curse of the Gur-Emir Mausoleum

In 1404, Tamerlane built an elaborate mausoleum for a favorite grandson who died young. It was called the Gur-Emir mausoleum, or "emir's tomb" (*emir* is Arabic for "ruler" or "commander"). After Tamerlane's death, his family buried him there as well, and other notable descendants were later buried there. In June 1941, Samarkand was part of the Soviet Union, and Soviet scientists came to the mausoleum to open the graves inside. According to a local legend, residents told the scientists not to touch Tamerlane's ashes; if they did, the people claimed, war would break out. The scientists ignored the warning, and Germany invaded the Soviet Union just a few days later. Famous for its architecture Gur-Emir today is a popular tourist attraction in Samarkand, which is now in Uzbekistan. The Uzbek government has also honored Tamerlane, erecting statues of him during the 1990s.

Tamerlane's tomb in Samarkand.

range of countries. Like the Mongols, Tamerlane demanded strict discipline from his troops. They were trained to follow orders communicated by the beat of a large drum. To win loyalty, Tamerlane shared the wealth he collected through conquest. He wrote (as quoted by David Nicolle in *The Mongol Warlords*), "To encourage my officers and soldiers I have not hoarded gold or jewels for myself. I admit my men to my table and in return they give me their lives in battle. I give generously and share in their sufferings. . . ." Some men who showed extreme bravery or skill were made *tarkhans*. As a *tarkhan*, a soldier did not have to pay taxes and could see the emperor without asking for permission.

In his government, Tamerlane kept many of the old titles that had been used in the Ilkhanate and Ulus Chaghatai. Two sets of officials, one Persian and one Turko-Mongolian, carried out the empire's policies. Both sets handled military and political affairs, although the Persians focused mostly on political events in the sedentary parts of the empire. Tamerlane used government positions to reward the ruling classes in the lands he conquered. These jobs gave the local officials power and a source of money–and strengthened their loyalty to Tamerlane.

The most important function of the government was collecting taxes, both tributes or taxes on wealth. Tamerlane, like all rulers, needed money to support his army and a lavish lifestyle. His government, like the khanates before it, taxed goods carried along the Silk Road and other trade routes. Another key job of high-ranking Persians and Turko-Mongols was making sure the local officials beneath them did what they were told. In some cases, Tamerlane let local governors stay in power after he defeated them, while royal officials collected taxes for the empire.

The Empire After Tamerlane

With his victories, Tamerlane held power over all or almost all of the old Mongol khanates. In 1404, he set his sights on the greatest prize: Khubilai Khan's old empire of China, now ruled by the Chinese Ming Dynasty. Tamerlane began assembling a huge force to march east, but he died the next year before setting out on his conquest. With Tamerlane's death, the Turko-Mongol princes of the Ulus Chaghatai and their allies competed for power. The foreign conquests ended during this era of civil war, which at times featured different rulers taking control in different parts of the empire. Finally, in 1409, Tamerlane's son Shahrukh (1377–1447) emerged as the next supreme leader of his father's lands.

Based in Herat, Shahrukh controlled Khurasan, while his son Ulugh Beg (1394–1449) ruled for his father in Transoxiana. When Shahrukh died in 1447, Ulugh Beg took control of the entire empire. Unlike Tamerlane, Shahrukh did not see the need to claims ties to Chinggis Khan and his descendants. Shahrukh stopped his father's practice of naming a member of the Mongol family as the supposed leader of the realm, and he took on the Arabic title of sultan, or king.

Once Shahrukh firmly established his control, the empire was relatively peaceful. But soon after Timur's death, local princes in Azerbaijan and present-day Iraq had won their independence from the Timurids. Tamerlane's former empire would continue to shrink through the 15th century, although his descendants would form a powerful new state in India. And the Mongol influence would continue throughout Central Asia and in the distant lands that had once come under the Great Khans' rule.

ANIMALS OF THE ARMY

Under Tamerlane, as with the nomadic Mongols before him, the horse remained the most important animal used in combat. But Tamerlane also relied on other creatures to carry out his battle plans. To communicate over long distances, he used carrier pigeons, which flew with messages strapped to their legs. Tamerlane also was the first Turko-Mongolian emperor to use battle elephants, which had been used for centuries in parts of Eurasia.

PART II

SOCIETY AND CULTURE

Mongol Government and Society

Daily Life in the Mongol Empire

Art, Science, and Culture in Mongol Lands

CHAPTER 4

Mongol Government and Society

BEFORE THE RISE OF CHINGGIS KHAN, THE BASIC MONGOL social and political unit was the clan. A group of related families formed a clan, and their primary purpose was to work together to survive. Pastures were owned by the clan, not individuals. By the end of the 12th century, the clans began to form larger units called tribes. Blood ties–relationships within the clan and the tribes–determined a person's social standing. The ruling clan of the Mongol tribes, called Borjigid or Kiyad, considered themselves to be born from heaven. They were known as people of the "white bone," while commoners were people of the "black bone." The ruling clan decided who and when the tribes would fight and enforced tribal customs.

Tribes elected their leaders at *quriltais,* which were social feasts as well as political gatherings. Some historians suggest the *quriltai* was not a true election, since not every Mongol could vie for the top position. Leaders came from the most powerful clans within a tribe, and voters most likely affirmed the reality that one of these men had the skills and the power to run tribal affairs. The first tribal leaders may have been religious leaders, called shamans. By the time of Chinggis, the leaders were chosen for their military skills and their ties to noble families.

The leaders relied on *nökörs* to carry out tribal affairs. *Nökörs* moved from one leader to another, looking for the one who could offer them the greatest riches or military power. *Nökörs* also acted as personal servants and bodyguards for their leaders. Their greatest service came during military campaigns. Leaders, especially the khans, built loyalty among their *nökörs* by giving them booty from conquests or from taxes collected in the foreign lands the Mongols controlled.

OPPOSITE
Ancient Tradition
Mongolian horsemen ride during the opening ceremony of the Naadam, a festival in modern Mongolia that originated as part of the quriltai.

CONNECTIONS >>>>>>>>>>>>

An Enduring Tradition

The festivities that were part of the *quriltai* live on today in Mongolia, in celebrations called *naadam*. The largest takes place in the Mongolian capital of Ulaanbaatar in July on National Day, a public holiday; smaller *naadams* are held across the country during the summer. A *naadam* features archery, wrestling, and horse racing—sporting events with strong ties to the nomadic culture of the early Mongols.

Men, Women, and Slaves

Women normally did not take an active role in politics or the military, with a notable exception within the royal family. A khan's wife could serve as a regent, or temporary ruler, after her husband died and before the next Great Khan was elected. Some wives could also influence the khan's decisions. Khubilai Khan often heeded the advice of his wife Chabi (d. 1281). She was his favorite wife; Mongol khans usually had several separate households with a different wife in charge of each one. The Mongols looked outside their own clan for wives, which strengthened ties between the clans.

The Mongols also had people who were similar to slaves. Slavery played a more important role in sedentary societies, though, and did not form a large part of Mongol society. After a successful battle, Mongol commanders took their enemy's surviving relatives as *Ötögus bo'ols*. The *Ötögus bo'ols* could not leave the service of their masters, but they could own property. Over time some of these *Ötögus bo'ols* were treated like family members and others were able to become important members of society. A lower class of slaves, *bo'ols*, did not have the same opportunities to seek wealth or social influence. The *bo'ols* were often sold into slavery by their families. *The Secret History of the Mongols* reports that one hungry Turkic man sold his son into slavery for a "[morsel] from the flesh" of a dead deer.

The Rise of Imperial Government

Around 1185, Temüjin had earned the title of khan among his tribe. It took another 20 years for him to unite all the tribes of Mongolia and become the Great Khan, Chinggis. Once he attained that position, he created a new form of government to rule over such a large and ethnically diverse society. Most historians say Chinggis's rise as a great conqueror rested as much on his political skill as his military brilliance.

Under Chinggis, military commanders loyal to him replaced many of the old clan and tribal leaders. When Chinggis was named Great Khan, he divided his army into 95 groups with 1,000 soldiers each, and he required all healthy men to serve in the military. Among those tribes and clans that were hostile to him, he deliberately did not group the soldiers along tribal lines, as had always been the custom. The soldiers' families were also expected to follow the orders of his military commanders. A commander's son could inherit his father's position. A commander could also lose his job if the khan wanted a different commander in charge.

Chinggis also developed the *keshikten* (Mongolian for "those with favor"), who served as the imperial guard. The *keshikten* consisted of day guards, night guards, and archers. These special soldiers, as Chinggis said (quoted in *The Secret History of the Mongols*), "watch over my 'golden life.'" Along with protecting the Great Khan, the *keshikten* carried out his orders and made sure the troops were ready for battle. As the empire grew, the *keshikten* provided the staff for the royal government and often represented the Great Khan in distant lands.

The idea of group ownership of land did not end with the coming of the khans. Chinggis ruled the empire for his family, not just himself. The only difference from the old days was that his family's lands stretched across an empire, not just a few pastures in Mongolia. The land and the power to rule it comprised the *ulus*. The Persian historian Juvaini (as quoted by Peter Jackson in *The Mongol Empire and Its Legacy*) described this arrangement: "Although authority and dominion [seem to] belong to one man, namely whoever is nominated *khan*, yet in reality all the children, descendants, and uncles partake of kingship and property." That arrangement changed somewhat as separate *uluses* developed among Chinggis's sons, but within each khanate the royal family followed the traditional Mongol ideas of ownership.

Mongol Laws

By uniting the Mongol tribes, Chinggis created a new nation. The tribes, however, had a long history of conflict, and the Great Khan was determined to use his power to create order. Soon after receiving his title, Chinggis said (as quoted by Paul Ratchnevksy in *Genghis Khan: His Life and Legacy*), "Punish robbery within the nation and clean up deception. Execute those who have deserved death and impose fines on those who deserve such fines."

Chinggis ruled by decree–his rules and decrees had the force of law. For many years, modern Western historians wrote about a legal code, the Great Jasaq, that Chinggis created for the Mongols in 1206. The Great Khan's brother-in-law was made the chief judge, and he was in charge of

GOD'S CHOSEN ONE

The Mongol khans did not set up a theocracy (a government run by religious leaders), but religion often played a part in their political decisions. Chinggis based his authority, in part, on the idea that Eternal Heaven had chosen him to rule. After defeating the Kereits he said he was "protected by Everlasting Heaven" (as quoted in *The Secret History of the Mongols*). At the *quriltai* in 1206 that confirmed Chinggis as Great Khan, a shaman said that Eternal Heaven—Möngke Tenggeri in Mongolian—had chosen Chinggis to lead.

recording the laws and making sure they were followed. In recent years, however, some historians have begun to challenge the idea that Chinggis created the Great Jasaq all at once. There is no direct written evidence of this legal code, just the works of later historians, such as Rashid al-Din, who quoted what was supposedly in it.

Currently, we do not know for sure if the Mongols of Chinggis's time had a written legal code. They did, however, have unwritten tribal laws that endured into the khanate period. And many of Chinggis's decrees were written down as formal laws. Future khans compiled these decrees and added their own, making a body of partly written and partly unwritten laws.

What has been called the Great Jasaq dealt with areas such as military operations and foreign affairs. Since the army was so crucial to the Mongol Empire, the laws enforced strict military discipline. A soldier who did not stop to pick up a dropped bow or other equipment would be executed. Giovanni DiPlano Carpini noted (in *The Story of the Mongols Whom We Call the Tartars*) that "when the line goes into battle, if one or two or three or more flee from the squad of ten, all ten are killed. . . . Also, if one or two or more proceed daringly into the fight and the remainder of the ten do not follow, they are killed." The Mongols also had strict laws regarding politics. Anyone who tried to rule without first being elected at a *quriltai* was executed.

As in other cultures, the Mongol legal system also included taxation. When they were strictly nomads, the Mongol leaders took a share of their people's herds as a tax. As they began to rule over sedentary societies, the Mongols made each person pay a tax in goods or money. The Mongols also taxed trade, taking a percentage of the value of goods sold.

Since the *uluses* and wealth technically belonged to everyone in a khan's family, the Mongol rulers needed a way to make sure the wealth they acquired was divided evenly. The system created to do this was the *jarqu*. The khan and other clan leaders met at the *jarqu*, which handled all clan affairs, not just money matters. Officials called *jarquchi* carried out the distribution of wealth for the clan members. In defeated lands, the *jarquchi* also conducted a census of the local population. The official count was used to determine how much tax the region owed to the Great Khan, who shared the money with local rulers as well as his family.

The Role of Local Officials

In *The Story of the Mongols Whom We Call the Tartars*, Giovanni DiPlano Carpini wrote that Chinggis had one ultimate law that drove him and his

THE RULE OF VENGEANCE

During their early nomadic years, many Mongol feuds and wars resulted from vengeance —using violence to respond to a perceived offense or wrongdoing by a person or clan. In effect, the Mongols took the law into their own hands, because they did not have a government that would arrest and punish criminals. This idea remained during the early years of the empire, and a foreigner's personal insult to the Great Khan was sometimes used as an excuse to start a war.

family to conquer their neighbors: "The Tartars must subject the entire world to themselves and have no peace with anyone unless they submit to the Tartars. . . ." but once the Mongols began conquering foreign lands, they had to create new political systems and rely on the help of local officials. Chinggis used officials called *daruqachi* and *basqaqs* to rule for him in distant lands. They collected taxes, raised troops, and settled disputes between local officials and nobles. The *daruqachi* were usually Turkic peoples friendly to Mongol rule who were considered their equal because of their military service for the Great Khan. *Basqaqs* were local people chosen to work for the khan. They eventually played a prominent role in the affairs of the Golden Horde, since the Mongols in Russia never set up a strong central government. In the other *uluses*, the Mongols used existing political structures to help them run local affairs.

During the early years of the Mongol empire, one of the key foreign officials was Mahmud Yalavach (d. 1262), a Muslim from Khorazm. Under Chinggis, he served as a *basqaq*. Ögedei gave him control over all of China under Mongol rule. A series of *jarquci* and other officials served under him. His son Mas'ud Beg (d. 1280s) held a similar position in Turkestan, a region centered in the oasis cities of Central Asia. The early Mongol khans also relied on Uighurs and other Turkic people of Central Asia to staff their imperial courts. The governments that developed in Central Asia and Persia were mostly Turko-Mongolian, rather than purely Mongolian.

By the time of Ögedei's death in 1241, the Mongols had split their realm beyond Mongolia into three main provinces. This division was for political purposes, to ensure strict control over the settled people. (The provincial system did not include Russia, which was not yet advanced and wealthy enough.) After the empire began to split into separate khanates, the provincial system was used to divide China into smaller political units. This system begun by the Mongols was the basis for the division of provinces still used in China today.

Mongol Society in China

Khubilai Khan's empire in East Asia was the largest of the four successor states that emerged from the single Mongol empire. The Great Khan considered China the grandest prize of the Mongol Empire. Modern historians know more about it than the other khanates because of the detailed records the Chinese kept throughout their history. Khubilai's China also has drawn more Western interest because of the writings of Marco Polo and other Europeans who traveled there.

As both the emperor of China and the Mongol Great Khan, Khubilai blended the political systems of the two peoples. The overall political structure, however, was more clearly Mongol, with the government focused on tribal organizations. Khubilai relied on *jarquchi* and *daruqachi* to carry out their traditional functions, although many government officials and departments received Chinese names. Khubilai wanted to at least appear Chinese, in an effort to retain the loyalty of his conquered subjects.

Soon after the 1260 *quriltai*, some of Khubilai's Chinese advisors made suggestions on how to run his central government. Not surprisingly, they wanted to keep as many traditional Chinese structures as possible. Khubilai accepted some of their ideas concerning economics. The government, for example, issued paper money and kept control of certain key industries, such as mining. But the Great Khan rejected the idea that he should keep the examination system used to select civil servants—the government workers who carried out most daily activities.

The Chinese system was designed to ensure that the most talented people served in the government, regardless of family connections and no matter who was ruling. Candidates for the civil service sat for examinations, which tested their knowledge of Chinese history, literature, and philosophy. Those who passed the examinations received government appointments. The civil service was dominated by the ideas of Confucius, one of China's greatest thinkers. Khubilai, however, did not trust the followers of Confucius who dominated Chinese politics. He was more interested in selecting civil servants loyal to him.

Khubilai divided the people of his realm into four classes. At the top were the Mongols, followed by western and Central Asians, then the Jin of northern China. The Song of southern China were at the bottom. The first two groups provided most of the emperor's most trusted officials. The army was eventually split into three parts: a Mongol cavalry under Khubilai's direct control, a provincial cavalry led by local commanders, and a Chinese infantry.

Adopting a Religion

During the Yuan Dynasty, the Mongols embraced many Chinese traditions, including Buddhism. This statue of the Buddha of Compassion is from 14th-century China.

Khubilai also tried to make the government more efficient. He eliminated some departments and directed affairs through three main offices. The Secretariat handled most civilian issues, while the Privy Council addressed military affairs. The Censorate made sure local officials performed their duties. Khubilai set strict penalties for government officials who broke the law or did not meet his standards for hard work. A lazy official might be beaten. So would officials who took bribes or used government workers to help them in their private lives. Mongol dominance, however, was not consistent throughout China. Despite the systems he set up, Khubilai did not have much real control in the more remote provinces. And although he demanded obedience and honesty, his legal system was not as harsh as the ones under some earlier and later Chinese dynasties.

CONNECTIONS >>>>>>>>>>>>

Paper Money

The Chinese invented paper money several hundred years before the rise of Chinggis Khan. The Mongols, however, helped spread its use. Marco Polo wrote in *The Description of the World,* "[I]n almost all the kingdoms subject to [Khubilai's] rule none is allowed to make or spend any other money." The Ilkhanate introduced paper money in Persia, and Marco Polo's descriptions of it introduced the idea of paper money to most Europeans. (Ironically, the Ilkhans did not understand how the system worked and paper money was soon withdrawn there.) Today, just as in Khubilai's China, only the central government of a nation is allowed to print money.

Communications and Trade Within China

Within China, Khubilai relied on a communication system that was first developed by the Great Khan Ögedei in his *ulus* and eventually spread to the other khanates, called the *jam*. The *jam* used a series of military posts about 25 or 30 miles apart. Each post had horses and supplies provided by local citizens. A rider on official business, such as carrying information to or from the Great Khan, picked up a new horse as he reached each post. By changing horses often, a messenger could cover about 200 miles in one day. The *jam* was also used by diplomats and, at times, by merchants. Riders had to show proof that they were allowed to use the system. Officials or messengers working for the government carried a *gere'e*, or tablet of authority. This oval plaque was made of wood, silver, or gold.

The Mongols seem to have borrowed the idea of the *jam* from the Kitans, but used it on a much larger scale. Other Asian governments later copied the system, and during the 19th century the U.S. government tried something similar with its Pony Express mail service. Historian

David Morgan wrote in *The Mongols*, ". . . the *jam* system was probably the most effective of Mongol imperial institutions after the Army."

The roads constructed to speed riders along the *jam* also played an important role in Mongol China's commerce. Khubilai encouraged trade, since he could tax it, and groups of merchants called *ortoq* were allowed to use the *jam*. Mongol China relied on Islamic merchants from Central Asia to move goods in and out of the empire along land routes. They brought in such things as camels, horses, medicines, and spices, while Chinese merchants exported textiles, ceramics, and food.

Merchants also transported their goods by boat, sailing from such Chinese ports as Fuzhou and Guangzhou. There was overseas trade with South Asian nations, such as India and Indonesia, as well as distant Persia.

The Silk Road

For thousands of years, traders and travelers have passed along the Silk Road, which cuts across China and Central Asia, across hot deserts and through high mountain passes, to the Middle East. The road is actually a series of roads, and its name comes from the silk that was one of the most valuable products carried from China to the West. The Mongols actively promoted trade along the Silk Road, especially in silk.

A 14th-century map shows Marco Polo's journey along the Silk Road.

Boats also carried goods along China's many rivers. Khubilai Khan reconstructed and extended China's Grand Canal, which dates from about 486 b.c.e. The canal is about 1,200 miles long and runs from Beijing to Hangzhou; parts of it are still used today. The canal made it easier to transport grain and other foods from the interior of China to the capital of Khan-Baliq.

The Mongols in Persia

Effective Mongol control of Persia and neighboring lands came with the conquests of Hülegü and the creation of the Ilkhanate. The Mongols took over a government and society dominated by Islam, although there were large Christian and Jewish minority communities. The Quran, the Muslim holy book, set down the laws of Islamic society. Under Hülegü, Mongol laws became more important, though the local people continued to live under Islamic law as well. The Mongols' toleration of all religions weakened the role of Islam in the government, at least until the Ilkhans converted to that faith. Even then, some Mongol leaders sought a return to the traditional laws. In the early 14th century (according to David Morgan in *The Mongols*), one Mongol general told other Mongols that it was a "disgraceful and dishonorable act" to abandon the Great Jasaq of Chinggis Khan.

As in China, the Ilkhans used some of the existing political structure to impose their rule. Hülegü and his successors, however, were more likely to use native officials in top positions. The family of the Persian Baha al-Din Juvaini (d. 1253) produced several key officials who helped the Mongols govern. The Jewish doctor Sad al-Daulat (d. 1291) was another important non-Mongol official. Serving under Arghun in the late 13th century, he enforced tax laws, sometimes by using torture. The Persians disliked Sad al-Daulat because of these harsh tactics and because he was Jewish. He also gave out government positions to his friends and relatives. But the historian Wassaf (1264–1334) admitted (as cited by J. A. Boyle in *The Cambridge History of Iran*) that "his reforms led to the disappearance of oppression, robbery and thieving." Sad al-Daulat clamped down on government officials who stole public funds and made sure Muslims were tried under their own laws, not Mongol laws. Sad al-Daulat, like other officials, had to "implement the directives" of the Ilkhans while dealing with Mongol princes and generals, who wanted to collect their own taxes and otherwise dominate the regions where they lived.

While ruling their own lands, the first Ilkhans also had duties as part of the larger Mongol Empire. More so than the other *uluses*, the Ilkhanate

WOMAN WARRIOR

Almost all Mongol warriors were men, but one notable exception was Khutulun (dates unknown). She sometimes rode into battle next to her father Khaidu, who spent decades challenging Khubilai's authority in Central Asia. Khutulun was said to dare men who wanted to marry her, demanding that they prove they were stronger or more skilled in combat than she. Each opponent also had to bet 100 horses. Khutulun never did marry, and she eventually owned 10,000 horses.

Mongols in Persia
The Mongols besiege a city in the Ilkhanate, from a 14th-century Persian illustrated history. Eventually, the Ilkhanate rulers adopted Islam.

remained loyal to the Great Khan, at least until Ghazan took power. He seemed to make a break with the Mongols of East Asia when he dropped the title Ilkhan and took the Muslim title of sultan. He also removed the Great Khan's name from his coinage. The Ilkhans never again considered themselves part of a larger Mongol Empire. These changes may have been designed to win local support among the Persians and Arabs, though; the Ilkhanate continued to have good military and diplomatic relations with the Great Khan.

One link between the Ilkhanate government and the court of the Great Khan was a Mongolian official named Bolad (c. 1240–1313). His family belonged to one of the Mongol tribes that came under Chinggis's rule before Chinggis became the Great Khan. Khubilai chose Bolad to be his ambassador at Tabriz, the Ilkhanate capital, and Bolad arrived there in 1285. For almost 20 years, he loyally served the different Ilkhans who came to power. He was a chief advisor for Arghun and also served the Ilkhanate on the battlefield. Bolad helped strengthen the Persian Mongols' ties to their traditional culture.

Changes Under Ghazan

The Mongol traditions weakened under Ghazan, as his conversion to Islam, and forced conversion of others (see page 40), led to a greater Muslim influence among the ruling class. The government, however, was not always united, and followers of the two main branches of Islam later struggled for influence.

One of Ghazan's major domestic goals was reforming the government's impact on the local economy. By some accounts, Mongol rule in Persia had led to cruelty and mismanagement. In some cities, Mongol raids had left half of all the homes empty, the residents dead or forced to flee. Taxes on commerce made it difficult for the towns and cities to rebuild. Ghazan wanted to fix tax rates so everyone knew what they owed and local princes could not demand higher payments for themselves. He also introduced a new coinage system and tried to improve the jam message system, which was similar to the one used in China. Ghazan encouraged farmers to return to land that had been abandoned, and he tried to improve the system for paying the army. He gave his commanders land that was supposed to be used to support the troops. In the Islamic world, rulers and other wealthy people sometimes create a *waqf*, which sets aside revenue from land or a business enterprise to maintain mosques and for charitable works. Ghazan created new land *waqfs* and used the money to help the elderly and sick.

Some historians believe Ghazan's changes did have some positive effect, especially in improving peasants' lives. Others, however, are not sure how deeply the reforms truly changed life for the overtaxed peasants. And after Ghazan's death, the Mongol princes who had lost power because of his reforms once again resumed control, leading to more economic stress.

As in China, Ilkhanate merchants took part in a vast trade network that linked Asia with Europe and North Africa. Some towns were famous for specific products: Shiraz, for example, was a center for iron works and wool weaving, while Isfahan was noted for its silk and cotton. (Both cities are located in modern-day Iran.) Other cities prospered with markets, called bazaars, set up to take advantage of the Mongols' movement between summer and winter camps.

Politics and Society in Mongol Russia

Before the Mongol invasion of Russia, the cities and towns were dominated by local princes. Nobles called boyars served the princes, and some boyars, in turn, had their own personal military and political aides, but these men did not owe loyalty to their boyar's princes. The Russians did not have any concept of a single powerful emperor, as in China and Persia. This local political system largely remained intact after Batu's conquest and the coming of the Golden Horde.

Batu and his successors were seeking tribute and were not concerned with having direct control over Russian lands. As steppe

CONNECTIONS >>>>>>>>>>>>

Great Grapes

Shiraz was a major Persian city before the Mongol conquests, and it is still an industrial center in Iran. The city's name is perhaps best known around the world for a type of grape that comes from there. Shiraz grapes are now commonly used to make fine wines.

dwellers, they did not want to live in the northwest forests. The Mongols controlled the steppe regions of their khanate, leaving the towns to the Russian princes. Focusing on the steppe also let them collect taxes on the trade that moved along the Silk Road and other caravan routes.

For the most part, the Mongols did not interact with the Russians, as they did with the local citizens of China and Persia. Their direct cultural contact was with the Kipchak nomads, a Turkic people of the steppes, where both peoples led a traditional nomadic lifestyle. One clear sign of the importance of Turkic culture among the Golden Horde turned up before the end of the 13th century. The Turkic language replaced Mongolian on the khanate's coins.

In the Russian towns and cities, the Mongols sent *basqaqs* to collect taxes, and Mongol soldiers protected them as they carried out their duties. The Mongols also recruited some local men to serve in their army; at times the "recruiting" could be violent, as Mongols forced Russians to serve. The Russians also had to pay for Mongol officials' food and housing. The Mongols based these taxes on the number of households, borrowing a system first developed in China. The Mongols also collected taxes on trade. An individual who could not pay taxes was forced into slavery. If the local people refused to pay tribute or rebelled against the Mongol officials, the khan quickly sent in large military forces from the steppes to reassert Mongol rule.

With their typical tolerance for all religions, the rulers of the Golden Horde did not make Russia's Orthodox Church pay taxes. The leader of the Church sent representatives to Saray, to keep good relations with the khan, and the freedom from taxes helped the Orthodox Church grow wealthy. This arrangement, however, did not stop local priests from speaking out against Mongol rule, which was not Christian. One Russian chronicle from the late 13th century records several sermons by a bishop named

Precious Object

This 14th-century bracelet from the region ruled by the Golden Horde is decorated with gold leaf and turquoise. The Mongols in Russia were much more concerned with treasure than they were with ruling.

Serapion (d. 1275). Serapion (as quoted by Charles Halperin in *The Tatar Yoke*) called the Mongols "merciless heathen, having neither mercy for the young, for the weak and aged, nor for infants." Yet Serapion and other religious leaders believed the Russians had themselves to blame for this treatment; the Mongol conquest was God's way of punishing Russians for their sins.

The Russian princes kept most of their local power, but the Mongols never let the princes forget they owed their power to the khan.

CONNECTIONS >>>>>>>>>>>

The Language of Taxes

With their tax system, the Mongols introduced several new words into the Russian language. The Russian word for "money" (*denga*) came from the Mongol word *tamga*, a government seal that showed merchants had paid a tax on their goods. The Russian word for "customs house" (*tamozhina*), where taxes were collected, also came from the same Mongol word. These words are still used in Russia today.

The princes had to travel to the Golden Horde's capital of Saray or, until 1259, to Karakorum to receive a *yarlik*, a document that spelled out the princes' right to rule. Many princes seem to have made their wills out before they left, not knowing if they would survive the journey—or the meeting with their Mongol masters.

Despite the fear they may have had of their Mongol lords, the Russian princes used the Mongol conquest to their advantage. With his loyal service to Batu and Berke, Alexander Nevsky developed more power than other Russian princes, helping to build wealth for himself and his family. Princes could also use their ties to the Mongols to control their local populations. As Richard Pipes writes in *Russia Under the Old Regime*, "A prince . . . had merely to threaten with calling in the Mongols to secure obedience."

Some Russian princes also used violence to keep order. Mongol words related to punishment entered common use as the princes borrowed from their masters. A *nagaika* was a type of whip and *kandaly* were chains. These were both Mongolian words that entered the Russian language unchanged. Under the Mongols, the Russians had their first death penalty, and the khanates used it against disloyal princes.

Although the Golden Horde brought violence, Russians saw some economic benefits. With Mongol protection, Russian merchants could travel to the Caspian and Black Seas to trade with Persians and Turks. The Russians offered furs and grains, and the fur trade helped turn Moscow into a major city. Goods also flowed through the Golden Horde's lands on their way to Egypt. The commerce included glass, pottery, and slaves. As always, the Mongols encouraged international trade, since they collected taxes on it.

Starting in the 14th century, Moscow (also called Muscovy) developed into the center of Russian military and political power. Even after the princes of Moscow were able to throw off the Golden Horde, they kept some of the Mongol methods for collecting taxes, organizing the government, and running the army. The Mongol influence lasted until the late 17th century, when Peter the Great eliminated systems that were based on Mongol practices and replaced them with European methods of government.

The Mongols of the Ulus Chaghatai

Historians know less about the Ulus Chaghatai than the other Mongol khanates. The region remained mostly nomadic, and neither the Mongols nor the defeated local peoples kept detailed written records. Even the khanate's precise borders are unknown, although it included Transoxiana and Semireche (modern Uzbekistan, Tajikistan, Kyrgystan, and southeastern Kazakhstan), and western Xinjiang, which now forms the western part of China.

Chaghatai and his descendants did not take over a large, established empire, as the Mongols did in China and Persia. The Chaghatai khans did not have a true capital city and in general they ignored their empire's cities. When they held a *quriltai*, the Mongol leaders usually met in the city of Almaliq, in what is now Uzbekistan. The rest of the time, the leaders lived no-

Mongol Devastation

The wars of conquest and resulting Mongol control in the Ulus Chaghatai had varying effects on the cities of Central Asia. Some cities were sacked but eventually rebuilt during the peace that followed. The city of Merv, however, was one place that suffered tremendously. Located in what is now Turkmenistan, the city had once been thought to be the home of the first humans, and under Muslim rule it turned into a center of learning. The Mongols, however, massacred the city's residents, and the surrounding farmlands soon turned to desert. Today, the town of Mary sits on the site of ancient Merv, which never really recovered from its destruction.

madic lives along the Ili River, which flows from western China into Kazakhstan.

For the later decades of the 13th century, the Ulus Chaghatai was dominated by Khaidu, who was not a direct descendant of Chaghatai. He wanted to control lands that he believed belonged to his branch of Chinggis Khan's family, founded by Ögedei. Khaidu's influence forced the khanate into wars with other Mongols and sparked civil war within the *ulus* (see chapter 2). Still, he also brought some stability. He provided defense against non-Mongol nomads from the north, and rebuilt some cities.

The Ulus Chaghatai was not truly free of Khaidu's control until the reign of Du'a (d. 1307). Some historians call him the greatest khan of the *ulus*. He tried to introduce reforms similar to the ones Ghazan carried out in Persia. In general, the Chaghatai rulers followed the Mongol *jasaq* and traditional political ways, at least until the khans converted to Islam in the 14th century. Until that time, the Mongols mostly let the Muslims of Chaghatai do as they pleased, as long as they paid their taxes. Muslim governors, watched over by Mongol or Turkish officials, ruled in the sedentary areas of the khanate.

The Mongols of Central Asia wanted to convert some farmland of their *ulus* into steppe. Local officials convinced them that using the land for agriculture would lead to more tax revenue, so the Mongols largely abandoned the plan. Still, in some regions, this transformation did occur. Shihab al-Din al-Umari (d. c. 1348), a Syrian geographer, described what he saw on a visit to Turkestan (as quoted by Svat Soucek in *A History of Inner Asia*): "A person . . . finds the buildings still standing but devoid of humans except for some nomads and herders, without any agriculture . . . what is green there consists of . . . steppe vegetation, which nobody has sown or planted."

With its steppe lands and dominant nomadic values, the Ulus Chaghatai had less commerce than the other khanates. Most economic activity centered on the few cities that survived the original Mongol onslaught, such as Samarkand and Bukhara. Smaller towns also served as commercial centers, such as Almaliq and Besh-baliq. The Silk Road linked the khanate with the major trading centers of eastern and western Asia.

CHAPTER 5

Daily Life in the Mongol Empire

MONGOL LIFE IN THE TIME OF CHINGGIS KHAN FOCUSED ON the herd. Farming was almost impossible on the steppes, since rain was sparse and the weather was often harsh, and a family, tribe, or clan depended on its animals for the necessities of life. Herds needed to be moved around the steppes to ensure there was enough for them to graze on, which is why the Mongols were nomads. The Mongols' most important animals were sheep and horses. Sheep provided food (both meat and milk), wool for cloth, and fuel–their waste was dried and burned. The Mongols used the food and clothing that came from their sheep for themselves and as goods to trade with sedentary communities. The Mongols traded with farmers and merchants for grains, cloth, and luxury goods.

Horses were the main source of Mongol transportation and played a large role in the success of the Mongol army. Horses also provided milk, which, when fermented, became a mildly alcoholic drink called *kumiss*. With the riches of their empire, the khans also bought huge quantities of strong alcoholic drinks, such as wine made from grapes or rice. The Mongols drank them often, and some historians suggest that certain Mongol rulers died at an early age because of alcoholism.

In their original homelands, the Mongols spent their summers on the wide-open steppes, then moved into mountain valleys for the winter. The trip from one pasture to another might cover about 100 miles. If a pasture no longer provided enough grass for their grazing animals, the Mongols might attack other tribes or foreigners to take over their land.

On the steppes, the Mongols lived in tents called *gers*. (Europeans called them *yurts*.) Felt cloth made from sheep's wool was draped over a wooden frame. The gers were round, with a hole in the center that let in light and also served as a chimney. The floor was covered with animal skins. The room inside was split into two halves, one for men and one for women.

Gers were easy to set up and take down quickly, so they could be moved without much trouble. Carpini noted (in *The Story of the Mongols Whom We Call the Tartars*) that "whenever [Mongols] travel, whether to war or other places, they always take their homes with them." During the period of the empire, the Mongols also had larger *gers* that were set up on large wagons and transported intact. Some Mongols who lived closer to the Gobi Desert also used tents called *maikhans*. More rectangular than a *ger*, a *maikhan* used poles to hold up the felt covering. These tents were never used as living spaces. Instead, they were places for entertainment and other special functions.

Food and Clothing

Mongolian men and women wore similar clothes, starting with a robe called a *de'el*. The robe might be lined with fur for warmth, and was closed with a belt. The outer part of the robe was usually covered in silk. Poorer

Portable Housing

Some Mongolian families still move their herds from one pasture to another, and many still live in gers. Maikhans *are also used, often during festivals such as the* Naadam. Kumiss *is also still part of the diet, although today it is usually called* airag.

people lined their clothing with wool or cotton. Underneath the *de'el* Mongols wore pants and some kind of an undershirt. During cold weather, they wore overcoats made of felt or fur. On their feet they wore thick stockings and boots made of leather, or in very cold weather, felt.

The one main difference between male and female clothing was headgear. Wealthy women wore tall, fancy hats called *boqtas*, which were covered with feathers and pearls—hard-to-get trade goods. Carpini wrote (in *The Story of the Mongols Whom We Call the Tartars*) that only married women wore *boqtas*, making it difficult to tell an unmarried woman from a man, since she would not wear a *boqta* and the rest of her clothing was just like a man's. Men usually wore fur hats with flaps that covered the ears.

The basic Mongol food was

CONNECTIONS >>>>>>>>>>>>

No Barbecues

If the Mongols lacked fuel for a fire, they ate their meat raw, chopping it up and mixing it with garlic. The Mongol taste for raw meat led European chefs to name a dish for them, steak tartare, which uses raw beef that is finely chopped and mixed with spices.

For many meals, the Mongols roasted meat over an open flame, and they continued that tradition even as they mixed with Asia's sedentary cultures. But the Mongols did not introduce the so-called Mongolian barbecue, which is found in some U.S. restaurants today. In these restaurants, diners choose from a variety of meats and vegetables, which are then cooked in oil in a large pan. This style of cooking is actually a Chinese invention and has nothing to do with the Mongols. In China, the meat and vegetables are cooked in a special pot with a cone in the center that holds burning charcoal, and a ring around the outside filled with boiling flavored broth.

dairy products and meat, either from their herd or game animals such as rabbits and fowl killed during their hunts. To a lesser degree, men also fished. Some meat was dried in the sun, which preserved it and made it easy to eat while on horseback. Bones, with some meat still attached, were boiled in a broth called *shülen*. Later this term was used to describe a stew of broth and meat thickened with grains or beans. Plant foods included seeds, berries, fruit, and mushrooms.

Before the Mongol conquests, a typical meal did not vary much from boiled meat and dairy products, but the growth of the empire led to the introduction of new foods, many from the Turkic peoples of Central Asia. One Turko-Mongolian dish was a rich pastry similar to baklava, which features layers of nuts, spices, and sugar. The word *baklava* seems to come from the Mongol word *bakla*, which means "pile up in layers." Mongols may have introduced this sweet treat to the Middle East and other lands they conquered. The Mongols also developed a taste for dishes from China and Persia.

During the time of the khanates, the common people provided food for the royal family and other leaders. The commoners ate whatever crops they grew that did not go to the Mongol elite or foods they obtained from trading animals or furs. As for slaves, William of Rubruck, in his book *The Journey of William of Rubruck to the Eastern Parts of the World, 1253–1255, as Narrated by Himself*, wrote that they "fill their bellies with dirty water, and with this they are content." At times the slaves also caught rats or mice for their meals.

Men, Women, and Children

In daily life, Mongol men and women shared many duties, although each also had some specific chores. For example, women set up and took down the tents, sewed clothes, and turned milk into other dairy products, such as cheese and butter. When not at war, the men's most important duties were making tools and hunting. The men had to make their own military equipment, including saddles and stirrups, and they took care of the horses.

Mongol men often had many wives, sometimes capturing women from neighboring tribes. Chinggis Khan was said to have had hundreds of wives, although he always remained very close to his first wife, Ö'elün. Families arranged marriages between their young children. Parents from the ruling class did this to create political bonds that would last for generations. The young Chinggis acquired his first wife this way when he was only nine years old, although the actual marriage ceremony took place years about six years later. Following a Mongolian custom, Chinggis—still known as Temüjin at this time—was left with the parents of his future wife.

Before the empire was built, Mongol children did not go to school. The Mongols did not have a written language until Chinggis introduced one much later, so they did not need to learn how to read or write. Sons and daughters learned the skills they needed from their parents. For sons, the most important skills were hunting and archery. Daughters watched their mothers carrying out the typical women's chores. Education changed as the Mongol rulers interacted with the cultures of Persia and China. The wealthy hired tutors to teach their children how to read and speak the native languages, while the poor continued to teach their young the skills they needed for adulthood.

Life in the Conquered Lands

Conditions for Europeans and Asians who came under Mongol rule depended on many things. People who had skills the khans needed were gen-

BLOOD BROTHERS

The young Chinggis Khan had a "blood brother." When he was 11, Temüjin and a friend exchanged gifts, marking their commitment to one another. Nomadic blood brothers also mixed a few drops of their blood in a glass and drank from it, although there is no record Temüjin did this. These choices were made by the young men themselves, but for the Mongols, choosing a blood brother was not merely child's play. Taking a blood brother created an *anda*, a relationship that united two men as political and military allies through their adulthood.

erally treated well. The poor and unskilled faced the same kind of difficult conditions they endured under local emperors and princes. Throughout the world in the 13th and 14th centuries, most rulers saw the peasant class as a source of taxes and resources, not as citizens with rights. This period is sometimes called the end of the medieval age, a time when most people in Europe and Asia lived in poverty and kings and princes dominated society.

In China, as noted in chapter 4, Khubilai Khan set up four classes of citizens. The Mongols were clearly the ruling class, though they made up just a small percentage of the population. Khubilai drew most of his advisors from the second class, the foreigners. The bottom two classes, the northern and southern Chinese, provided most of the money and labor the Great Khan needed for his government.

Khubilai forced Chinese peasants to build his palaces and such projects as the Grand Canal. Yet he also tried to help the Chinese farmers. After the Mongol wars of conquest, the peasant farmers' lands had been destroyed. Khubilai forbid the Mongols from grazing their animals on the farmland that remained, so the peasants could survive—and help feed the empire. Khubilai helped other farmers by lowering taxes, and he gave out grain to poor Chinese who could not afford to buy food.

In rural areas, the Mongols preserved the traditional Chinese *she*, a system that united 50 farming families into one group. Working together, the government thought, the farmers could more quickly reclaim damaged land and increase their crop production. Southern farmers focused on rice and tea, while northern farmers raised barley, wheat, and cotton. Chinese farmers also raised fruits and vegetables, and some grew mulberry trees, which were used to feed the worms that produce silk.

The Ruling Class

The Mongols were the ruling class in Chinese society, although they made up just a small part of the population. This 13th-century Chinese woodcut shows a Mongolian general.

An International Society

Under Khubilai Khan, Chinese society took on an international flavor—probably more so than in any other nation at that time. The Mongol conquests had touched many countries and peoples, and Khubilai welcomed to China anyone who could help him develop his empire. Most numerous were Turkic peoples and Muslims of Persia and Central Asia. His army also included Alans, steppe dwellers from southern Russia who belonged to the Orthodox Church. Marco Polo was the only European known to serve Khubilai, but under earlier Great Khans, Europeans artisans worked in Central Asia. These included William Boucher, a goldsmith from France. He is best known for designing a fountain that sat in the palace of Karakorum. Shaped liked a tree, the fountain poured out wine and *kumiss*.

The *she* also gave rural dwellers some of their first schools, where young boys learned farming skills and the basics of reading Chinese.

Khubilai Khan also needed the skilled workers and merchants in the cities for his empire to thrive. Artisans, such as jewelers and weavers, received food and clothing from the government and could sell some of their goods on the open market. Merchants benefited because the Mongols welcomed trade. Traditional Chinese rulers considered buying and selling goods an unworthy profession and saw merchants as greedy. The Mongols helped merchants by freely loaning them money and removing an old Chinese restriction on how much profit they could make. Under Mongol rule, cities bustled with economic activity; Marco Polo often described the number of merchants, foods sellers, and artisans he saw at work. Of the city of Quinsai (modern Hangzhou, on the east coast of China), he wrote (in *The Description of the World*), " . . . on every market day all the . . . squares are covered and filled with people and merchants who bring [goods] on carts and on boats, and all is disposed of."

Life in the Ilkhanate

The early decades of Mongol rule in Persia and neighboring lands brought great changes to the local people—most of them bad. The region was mostly sedentary, though some nomadic Turks had already ruled there before the Mongols. Warfare and the Mongol policy of trying to convert farmlands to pastures destroyed the agricultural economy. As in China, the local population greatly decreased during the early years of Mongol rule. Many people were forced into slavery, and one historical account says that after the conquests, the survivors in the region of Balkh in northern Afghanistan could only find dogs, cats, and human flesh for food.

Before the invasions, the people of Persia had a healthy economy. Farmers produced corn, rice and other grains, fruits, and vegetables, as well as cotton and silk. Under the Mongols, until the rule of Ghazan at the end of the 13th century, farmers struggled to make their fields productive again. His tax relief and other programs helped the farmers, although agricultural output did not rebound to the levels it had reached before the Mongols arrived. Peasant farmers did not have the freedom to live and work where they chose. The government forced them to stay on the land where their families had always lived. And, as in China, peasants might be forced to do construction work at no pay, which further impeded their efforts to farm the land.

By the mid 14th century the local people were once again growing a variety of crops. Melons were grown everywhere, with many sent abroad. Fruits in general were a major part of agriculture, while vegetables were mostly grown near larger cities. The fruits included figs, lemons, peaches, pears, and oranges.

City life in Persia felt the same harsh effects of the Mongol conquest. The early Mongol policy of heavily taxing trade slowed the rebuilding of some cities. Others, however, managed to do well, especially after Ghazan cut some of the taxes on trade. A typical city dweller might do craft work, such as making clothes, ceramics, or carpets; artisans in the same craft often lived and worked together in a particular section of a city. Other city residents helped transport or store goods that were traded with foreign cities. Local residents also earned money working for the Mongols, who had several different camps throughout the khanate.

The most powerful local people in Persia were the landlords and officials. They usually owned land outside the cities, but they began to take a more active interest in trade during Mongol rule. The landowners and the wealthy merchants formed the upper class, with artisans and peasants at the bottom.

The influence of Islam on Persian society endured under Mongol rule. Schools called *madrasas* taught both religion and Islamic law, usually

ONE ROSY PICTURE

One Persian industry that prospered during Mongol times was growing flowers for their oils. These oils were used to create a variety of medicines and perfumes. The oil of roses was used to make rose water, which helps moisten dry skin. Today parts of southern Iran are still known for their rose water.

just to boys. (*Madrasas* for both boys and girls exist today in Muslim countries.) Still, under the khans, non-Muslims found they had greater social and political influence than in the past.

Life in the Golden Horde

As noted in chapter 4, the rulers of the Golden Horde did not play a role in the everyday affairs of their Russian lands. Their most direct contact was with the Russian officials who collected taxes and the princes who ruled local areas. The Mongols' greatest contact was with the Turkic people who had moved into Russia before the Mongol conquests.

The Russians in the towns of the east were Slavs, related to other Slavic people of Eastern Europe. For the average people of Slavic Russia, life did not change much under Mongol rule—unless they were forced into the military. Farming was never easy in the forests around the upper end of the Volga River. Peasants who cleared away trees then had to deal with short summers and bad soil. Families hunted and fished to make sure they had enough food, and lived in log cabins made from the trees they cut. A typical rural home included three generations of the same family: grandparents, their adult children, and the adults' children.

Farther south along the river the farming was better, and the area where the Volga meets the Oka River, near Suzdal and Vladimir, drew many Russian settlers. That area remained a main source of wheat under Mongol rule. Land was the main source of wealth in the isolated regions of Russia, and families with large farms used slaves or peasants to work the land for them. In general, the peasants were not tied to one plot of land; they could move on and work for a different landowner if they chose. If they owed a landowner money, however, the peasants could not leave, and the owners tried to make sure the peasants remained in debt.

Novgorod, Russia's only large city at the time, was a thriving trade center. At the city's peak in the 13th century, its merchants traded furs and hemp in Europe for wine and cloth. The Mongol capital of Saray also developed a strong economy. Many city residents worked smelting iron and turning it into finished products. Remains of clothing shops and jewelers have also been found by archaeologists on the site of the city.

In some ways, Russians benefited under the Golden Horde. Foreign trade increased as Russia joined the international trade network the Mongols supported. The Mongol presence also helped unite the Russians and create a sense of being Russian, of having a national identity, and not merely being the subject of the local prince. The Russian Orthodox

Church played a part in creating this nationalism. It was the only native, central power in the land, and the people looked to church leaders and their own faith for the strength to endure the foreign invaders. Recent historians have also questioned the idea, held by earlier historians, that the Mongol conquests totally disrupted life across Russia. In *The Crisis of Medieval Russia*, John Fennell writes, "things returned to normal, or near-normal, in a remarkably short time."

Nomadic Life in the Ulus Chaghatai

Daily life in the khanate of Chaghatai most resembled the life the Mongols knew in their homeland. Most of the conquered people were nomadic Turks, so they shared many cultural similarities with the Mongols. Over time, the Mongols completely blended in with the Turks, leading to the creation of a new language, called Chaghatai Turk. Their nomadic culture remained basically unchanged, except for the adoption of Islam as the major faith in the mid-14th century.

Not all the natives of Central Asia were strictly nomads. Some were semi-nomads: They kept a base camp or village but moved out to farther pastures during part of the year. At their permanent homes, the semi-nomads farmed, and women wove colorful bags and carpets. The bags could be used to carry items or decorate the walls of a *ger*.

Since the Mongols of Central Asia remained true to their nomadic roots, they largely ignored the cities in their midst. But in such places as Samarkand and Bukhara, the local people lived typical urban lives of the time. The cities, although heavily damaged during the Mongol conquests, slowly rebuilt their schools and marketplaces.

Religion in the Mongol Empire

Across Europe and Asia, religion played a huge role in political and daily life throughout the medieval period—not because of the Mongols themselves, but because the various parts of the Mongol Empire were dominated by Christianity (in Russia), Islam (in Persia), and Buddhism (in China). The different religions shaped the Mongol khans' personal lives and their political decisions. The local khan's faith sometimes determined what laws were enforced and who was considered an enemy. And some religious leaders labeled anyone who did not follow their faith "heathens," and used religious difference as a reason to wage wars.

The Mongols' original religious beliefs centered on ancestor worship. They kept images of their dead relatives and prayed to their spirits.

CIVIL WARS

Although the Russians may have had some sense of nationalism under Mongol rule, the Russian princes continued to fight among themselves for power. During the 1280s and 1290s, princes from the same family sometimes battled each other, trying to win control of larger regions. At one time, Mongol forces fought against each other during these Russian wars, as Noghai and Tode Möngke backed rival princes.

Shamans Today

Shamanism developed across Central Asia and Siberia, and the "medicine men" of North and South American Native peoples are also shamans. Shamanism is still practiced around the world today, including in Mongolia, although Tibetan style Buddhism is now the dominant religion. Shamanistic powers are thought to pass from parents to their children. Stanley Stewart, in *In the Empire of Genghis Khan: A Journey Among Nomads*, described a session with a shaman who entered a trance and made predictions about the future. The shaman told Stewart that contacting the spirits is not easy: "I am often afraid. The way to the spirits is littered with the souls of fallen shamans."

Ancestors could become spirits of mountains and water. Above all these spirits was Eternal Heaven (Möngke Tenggeri). Earth was seen as an ancient grandmother.

In the time of Chinggis, the Mongol religion was shamanistic: The people looked to religious leaders called shamans to offer religious guidance. The shamans were mostly men, but some were women. Shamans, the Mongols believed, had the power to communicate with gods and spirits. The shamans were the link between the world of humans and the supernatural. They could drive out evil spirits and seek help from good ones. They usually performed their duties, such as praying, on hills or mountains, so they would be closer to heaven. Shamans could also use their skills to cure disease and, supposedly, to predict the future. When Chinggis was named Great Khan, the Mongol shaman said (as reported by Juvaini and quoted in Paul Ratchnevsky's *Genghis Khan: His Life and Legacy*), "God spoke to me, saying: 'I have given the whole Earth to Temüjin and his sons. . . . See that he rules justly!'"

At times, the Mongols sacrificed animals to the gods and spirits. To keep evil spirits out of their homes, they made strangers walk between two fires. The fires were thought to drive out any spirits occupying their guests, and they were also used to purify relatives who were inside a *ger* when a family member died. Carpini reported (in *The Story of the Mongols Whom We Call the Tartars*) that a Russian prince who refused to pass between the fires and then bow to a statue of Chinggis Khan was trampled to death.

Modern historians suggest that the Russian prince was killed because of a political disagreement with the Mongols, not for rejecting a practice of their religion. When it came to religious beliefs, the Mongols were perhaps the most tolerant people in the medieval world. In general, they readily accepted other peoples' gods, while often still following their shamanistic traditions.

Christianity

Even before Chinggis united the Mongol tribes, the Mongols had some contact with other faiths, primarily Christianity and Buddhism. The Christians in Mongolia belonged to the Church of the East, formed by the Assyrian people in what is now Iraq. European Christians called them Nestorians. The Assyrian Christians described the interrelation of human and divine natures of Jesus Christ somewhat differently than other Christians did. In church, they used the Syriac language, which is closely related to Aramaic, the language Christ spoke.

During medieval times, the Church of the East spread across Asia; it was the first form of Christianity to reach India and China. Some Mongol tribes embraced it, and later members of Chinggis's family were Christians, including the wives of Hülegü and Tolui. When the European missionary William of Rubruck reached Karakorum in 1254, he met with these "Nestorians" and noted they had their own church in the capital city. During the 1280s, the head of the Assyrian Church was based in the Ilkhanate, and the Mongol leaders sometimes turned to him for advice. The growth of the Church of the East and reports from Assyrian priests led some Europeans to believe the Mongol khans had become Christians, or were at least considering it.

Through conquest and diplomacy, the Mongols made their first contact with other forms of Christianity in the medieval era, Roman Catholicism and Eastern Orthodoxy. Catholicism, led by the pope in Rome, dominated Western and Central Europe. The Eastern Church was centered in Constantinople, and its focus was on Eastern Europe, including Russia, and parts of the Middle East. Differences between the two sometimes led to political conflicts between rulers of the different faiths. These conflicts increased during the Crusades, which began in the 11th century and lasted for several hundred years. During this series of wars,

The Myth of Prester John

The presence of Christians in China and Central Asia gave rise to a powerful myth in medieval Europe. Many Europeans believed that a great Asian king named Prester John was a Christian who would come to the Middle East and help the Crusaders defeat the Muslims. Marco Polo associates the mythical Prester John with Toghril, a real Christian prince of the Church of the East from Mongolia. In his *Travels*, Polo spends several chapters describing a war between Ong-khan and Chinggis. Prester John was also associated with an earlier Central Asian ruler, Yelu Dashi (1087–1143), who founded the Kara-Kitay Empire during the 12th century.

The Orthodox Church in Russia

The Russian Orthodox Church did not have to pay taxes under the Mongols, and became increasingly influential. However, the Golden Horde never embraced Christianity. The onion-shaped domes on this 18th-century wooden church are typical of Russian Orthodox architectural style.

Catholic soldiers and their leaders fought for control of lands in the Middle East that bordered the major Orthodox nation, the Byzantine Empire. Political and religious differences kept the Catholics and Orthodox Christians from uniting to fight their common enemy, the Muslims.

The first Christians the Mongols fought were in Georgia, during Chinggis's western campaign of the early 1220s. The Europeans regarded the Mongols as pagans seeking to dominate the world. By the time the Mongol Empire was firmly established across Asia, the Roman Catholics of Europe began sending ambassadors and missionaries to Karakorum and other parts of the empire.

In 1245, Pope Innocent IV (1243–1254) sent the priest Giovanni DiPlano Carpini to Mongolia on a diplomatic mission. The monk met both Batu and Küyük. Neither was interested in converting, but these and other khans were welcoming to the Christians who came to their lands as both diplomats and missionaries. By about 1275, the Catholic leaders of Western Europe, who knew that Asian armies with Christian ("Nestorian") troops were advancing westward, had become more friendly and hoped these forces were led by Prester John (see page 89) and would help them fight the Muslims.

The Golden Horde dealt primarily with the Russian Orthodox Church, a branch of Eastern Orthodoxy. As noted in chapter 4, the Russian church did not have to pay taxes under Mongol rule. In return, the priests were expected to pray for the Mongol leaders and their families. Still, the Mongols leaders never embraced Orthodox Christianity (or Roman Catholicism) the way they did other faiths they encountered during their conquests. In their first years in Russia, the Mongols remained separate from the Russians and their church, choosing to follow their traditional beliefs.

Buddhism

Buddhism, which was developed in India more than 2,500 years ago, is based on the teachings of the Buddha ("enlightened one"), a prince who gave up his wealth to try to understand the meaning of life and death. The Buddha's beliefs were based on Indian religious teachings, which stressed reincarnation. When a living being dies, according to Buddhism, its essence lives on and is reborn in another person or animal. The Buddha, however, went beyond this, setting down what he called the Four Noble Truths: 1. All existence is suffering. 2. The cause of suffering is desire, which is fueled by ignorance of the reality of the world. 3. There is a way to end ignorance and suffering, by severing attachments to objects and feelings. 4. The way to end desire is to follow the Buddha's eight rules for right living. The goal of Buddhism is to help people stop the endless cycle of life, death, and rebirth. When Buddhists end this cycle, they say they are enlightened, just like the Buddha, and they have reached a state of existence called nirvana.

Buddhism existed in China for hundreds of years before the rise of the Mongols. At different times, it was the country's official religion. The first form of Buddhism to spread among the Mongols was Chan, which is the Chinese version of the Zen Buddhism still practiced in Japan and other nations. Under Khubilai Khan, Buddhism received strong imperial support, although following Mongol custom, the Great Khan did not proclaim it the state religion. Khubilai's Buddhism, however, was not Chan or other forms commonly practiced in China. He turned to Tibet for religious inspiration. Tibetan Buddhism is sometimes called Lamaism from the word *lama*, which means "teacher" in Tibetan.

In China, the Buddhists battled for influence at Khubilai's court with the followers of a native Chinese religion, Daoism. Daoism is based on the teachings of the philosopher Laozi, and also has some elements of magic and fortune telling. In the end, the Buddhists won, and one of Khubilai's most important advisors was the Phags-pa Lama (1235–1280). The lama helped Khubilai win favor among China's Buddhists by associating the Great Khan with Buddhist holy figures. Khubilai then banned the practice of Daoism.

During the peak years of their empire, the Mongols helped spread Buddhism to other parts of Asia. The Ilkhanate's first rulers, particularly Arghun, supported Lamaism and erected Buddhist temples. But just as in China, Buddhism was never an official religion, since the Ilkhans followed the Mongol policy of tolerating all faiths—that is, until Ghazan banned Buddhism (see page 40).

Islam

As the Mongols moved westward across Asia, the dominant faith they met was Islam; the Middle East and parts of Central Asia were ruled by Islamic leaders. The religion had developed during the seventh century under its founder, Muhammad. Muslims believed he was the last prophet sent by God, and his teachings became both religious and civil law. The Muslims believed in the same god the Jews and Christians did, but Muhammad said only people who accepted his own teachings regarding God's word were true followers of Allah (the Arabic word for God).

Muhammad and his followers won a series of wars that helped Islam spread from its starting point in Mecca, in what is now Saudi Arabia. In the lands they conquered, Muslims allowed Christians and Jews to practice their faith, but they did not tolerate other religions. The Muslims believed they had a holy mission to place the entire world under Islamic rule. Their conquests, however, had largely stopped by the time the Mongols rose to power in Asia. The coming of the Mongols marked the first time large Islamic populations were not governed by fellow Muslims.

The khans of the Golden Horde were the first to convert to Islam, even though the religion was not particularly strong in Russia. Eventually all the khanates except Yuan China were mostly Islamic. As the Mongols converted, shamanist practices continued, though over time the traditional beliefs died out.

Islamic Mongols
This 13th-century Quran comes from Iran. Eventually all the khanates, except the one in China, were mostly Muslim.

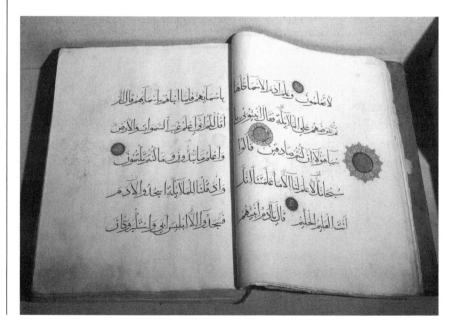

In Persia, the Mongols eventually saw value in sharing the same religion as the largest part of the population. They kept the traditional Muslim tolerance of Christians and Jews, but believers of other faiths, such as Buddhism, lost their freedom of religion. Almost all traces of Buddhism in Persia were destroyed once the Ilkhans converted to Islam. Ahmad Tegüder was the first Ilkhan to convert. Since him every ruler in Persia (and now Iran) has been a Muslim. Öljeitü, the next Mongol Ilkhan after Ghazan, embraced the Shiite branch of Islam, leading to its spread in Persia. Today, Iran's rulers and most of its citizens still follow Shiism. The Mongol conversion in Persia and elsewhere led many Mongols to embrace the native Islamic cultures and lose their distinct Mongol traditions.

The khans of the Ulus Chaghatai were the last to convert to Islam. The first one to do so, Tarmashirin (d. 1334), angered other Mongols who still accepted shamanism. At a *quriltai*, the Mongol princes forced him from power, saying he should not have replaced Mongol laws with Islamic laws. By the end of the 14th century, however, the khans of Central Asia had accepted Islam.

Judaism in the Mongol Empire

Mongol contact with Judaism came through their conquest of Islamic lands. Jews had lived in such cities as Baghdad for generations, and sometimes held important positions. Jews (and Christians) who converted to Islam had the greatest chance of success under the Islamic Empire, and later under the Mongols. One prominent Jew during Mongol times was Rashid al-Din, a convert to Islam. He was trained as a doctor, as were many Jews in Islamic lands, but served the Ilkhanate as an advisor. He is best known today as a historian, and his books on Mongol history are still read.

فلما سمع ذلك الفيل أعجب به فانطلق معه هلم إلى العين فأوى وعندها

فأراه ظل القمر ففعل الفيل ذلك فاضطرب الماء وتحرك ظل القمر فيه فقال انظر إلى

غضبه فقلت تخوف ذلك واشفق منه وقال لست عائداً ولا آخذاً من الفيلة

صورة الفيل غايص في العين وظل القمر العين والأرنب مرتفعة تنظر وتخاطب الفيل

وإنما ضربت لكم هذا المثال لأن البوم شديد العداوة شديد لا يستطاع

الدنو منه ولا المشاورة وله نجوم وحملة وكثرة شر وكسر الملك ولا

CHAPTER 6

Art, Science, and Culture in Mongol Lands

THROUGHOUT CIVILIZATION, THE GREATEST ACHIEVEMENTS in arts and science have come from cultures that were settled in one place. In early societies that were based on agriculture, the people eventually developed farming methods that enabled fewer workers to produce enough food for everyone. More people then had time to do other things, such as pursue arts and crafts, write literature, educate others, and develop science and technology.

Because nomads such as the Mongols keep moving, carrying all their belongings with them, they do not create museums or universities. Certainly, though, they must master many artistic and scientific skills, and they certainly have a rich heritage of culture and learning. And as the Mongols proved, once nomadic peoples conquer cities, they can appreciate the value of other cultures' artistic and intellectual achievements.

Mongol Arts

Thousands of years before the Mongol tribes settled in Mongolia, people in the region painted scenes of everyday life on caves. These rock paintings, called *petroglyphs*, illustrate one of the earliest forms of nomadism. The earliest artists of Mongolia painted on rocks and other natural surfaces as well, and also created large monuments called deer stones. These stones ranged from about six to 30 feet high and featured carvings of deer and other animals. Historians believe the stones marked the graves of important leaders and warriors.

Other art items from the era before the Mongols include jewelry, pottery, and felt carpets. The Mongols made similar items, finding ways to decorate the tools they used in their everyday life. Clothes and other items featured embroidered designs symbolizing such things as fire or the artist's hopes for the future. About 7,000 of these symbols are known, and they still appear in modern Mongolian art.

The Mongols also made musical instruments and wrote songs, usually dealing with animals and aspects of nomadic life. The instruments included the *morin khuur*, a two-stringed instrument played with a bow. The first ones were made from horse skin and hair. The *morin khuur* was used to mimic the sounds of animals and nature. The Mongols also developed other string instruments and played drums and flutes. The earliest Mongol dances came out of the shamans' movements as they entered trances to reach the spirit world.

Singing and dancing were an important part of festivals. Folk dances were performed either inside or just outside the Mongols' *gers*. The limited space led to a dancing style that stressed moving the hands, head, and upper body and limited leg movements. Today Mongolians still dance in this way, even when they have more room to move.

The Mongols passed on their history and folk tales orally. Some proverbs date back at least to the times of the Huns, which ended around the fourth century. The first Mongol alphabet did not appear until 1206, when Chinggis Khan decided to use the script of the Uighur Turks. This script was already used by the Naimans, one of the tribes Chinggis defeated in Mongolia. Words were written from top to bottom, and sentences were read from left to right, as in English.

The only major piece of writing to survive from the empire is *The Secret History of the Mongols* (other writings have survived only in Persian or Chinese translations). Historians have debated whether it is pure fiction or a mixture of fact and fantasy. The beginning, for example, says that the first Mongols descended from a "bluish wolf" and a deer. Most historians, however, accept that *The Secret History* is probably accurate when it describes the events of Chinggis's life.

Historians continue to debate when *The Secret History of the Mongols* was written. The book's unknown author (or authors) says the book was completed in the year of the mouse. The Mongols, like the Chinese, based their calendar on 12-year cycles in which each year was named for a different animal. This calendar system is still used in many parts of Asia today. By examining other dates and events mentioned in *The Secret History*, historians believe that 1228, 1240, or 1252 are the most likely years of the mouse in which the book was written.

Mongol Technology

By studying nature, using trial and error, and borrowing from neighboring peoples, the Mongols created technology that made daily life easier. One example of this is the *ger*, a warm, comfortable, yet thoroughly portable house (see page 80). Among the greatest Mongol achievements, though, came in warfare, especially archery. The Mongols developed a bow made out of several layers of wood and animal horns. This bow required greater strength to pull than other bows of the time, but it remained flexible longer than other bows and shot arrows farther.

The Mongols also developed a wide range of arrows, each with a specific purpose. A short arrow was useful for hunting small animals. Heavy arrows were used against an enemy wearing armor or any time the arrow had to penetrate deep into its target. The Mongols also had a special "whistling" arrow that made noise in flight or when it struck its targets. These arrows were used for sending signals. Arrowheads were often made of bone, and here again the Mongols had different heads for different purposes. Small heads were good for entering hard surfaces, while wider heads created more damaging wounds when they struck game or enemy troops.

Monster Mask
Singing and dancing were important parts of Mongol festivals. Dancers wore masks and elaborate costumes to signify what character they played.

CONNECTIONS >>>>>>>>>>>>

Falconry Today

The Mongol fondness for falcons continues today, especially among the Kazakhs of Mongolia. These Turkic-speaking people live in the western part of the country. They continue to hunt with golden eagles, most likely the same type of bird Marco Polo saw snatching wolves off the ground. As hunters ride their horses, the birds sit on their arms. The eagles are so large and heavy, the riders use wooden poles to help their arms support the birds.

Hunting Skills

For Mongol men, hunting was an important part of survival. But among the elite, it also served as a form of recreation and a social event. Even as they settled in sedentary communities, the Mongols valued hunting as a recreational activity. In his summer capital of Shangdu, Khubilai Khan built an enormous hunting park. Surrounded by earthen walls, the park had streams and woods, and deer roamed the grounds. Khubilai also hunted in the wild, using trained lions and leopards to help him catch his game, which included boars, bears, and deer.

The Mongols also enjoyed falconry—using trained falcons to capture small game and other birds. Their trained birds included large eagles, as well. In his *Travels*, Marco Polo wrote, ". . . those especially that are trained to wolf-catching are very large and powerful birds, and no wolf is able to get away from them."

Chinese Culture and the Mongols

Before their conquests, the Mongols had contacts with China through trade and political alliances. The Chinese built their first empire almost 1,500 years before Temüjin earned the title of Great Khan. Throughout their history, the Chinese excelled at writing in many forms and styles, especially philosophy. Even before the first empire, a group of great thinkers set down rules of society and government that continued to influence China through Mongol times and beyond. The most important of these thinkers was Confucius. He taught that everyone had a specific role to play in society and should accept their position. Within the confines of this role, people were obligated to act morally. Just as a citizen had a duty to obey the rulers, the rulers had to govern fairly.

Confucius's ideas helped shape the system that trained government officials in China. As noted in chapter 4, Khubilai was suspicious of Chinese officials in his government, but Confucians still served the Mongols. These Chinese officials hoped they could make the Mongols accept Chinese culture and perhaps rule less harshly. The Confucians tried to teach Khubilai their beliefs, but his limited knowledge of Chinese made this difficult. Still, the Great Khan made sure his second son was schooled in Confucianism and other aspects of Chinese culture. To further link the Mongols with the Chinese and to help educate the Mongols, Khubilai had some Confucian books translated into Mongolian. Khubilai also approved the establishment of the National History Office to document Mongol rule in China.

Throughout China's rise to power as the dominant nation in East Asia, its rulers supported the arts. Under Khubilai and his Mongol successors, this support continued. Khubilai enjoyed theater and had plays staged at his royal palaces. Theaters also drew large crowds in China's cities during his rule. Yuan Dynasty theater often combined short plays or skits with songs and dancing. Theatrical performances might also include mime and acrobatic stunts.

Actors and other entertainers had higher social status under Khubilai than they had in the Jin and Song Empires. One Mongol general ordered (as quoted at the web site Yuan Drama, www.columbia.edu/~jv287/mongol/drama2.html) that "all the townspeople be put to death except artisans and entertainers." The Mongols also did not seem to limit what playwrights could show on stage. Under the old Confucian system, playwrights came from the class of educated government officials who had to take tests to demonstrate their grasp of Confucian ideals (see page 34). Khubilai ended the civil service examination system, and anyone could write and stage plays. Under Khubilai, playwrights and novelists also had greater freedom to use the language of everyday conversation, not the more formal language favored by native Chinese rulers.

During Khubilai's rule, more books appeared in China than during previous dynasties. K. T. Wu (quoted by Morris Rossabi in *Khubilai Khan: His Life and Times*) says that under the Mongols, "printing attained prominence from the standpoint of quantity if not quality and technique." In 1269 the Great Khan set up a government office to print books, and he later gave land to schools to use as a source of income, so they could publish texts. In general, however, the Chinese were

CONNECTIONS >>>>>>>>>>>

Enduring Creative Works

More than 150 plays written in China during Mongol rule still exist today, and at least three times that many were written but did not survive. The Mongol Theater of the Yuan Dynasty shaped the kinds of opera still performed in China today.

The Old Writing Returns

The Mongol script was used from the time of Chinggis until 1942. At that time, Mongolia was under the influence of the Soviet Union, and Soviet officials forced the Mongolians to write their language using the Cyrillic alphabet, which was first developed in Russia. By 1990, only about 10 percent of Mongolians, mostly elderly, could still read the Mongolian script. However, Mongolian script survived in a part of Mongolia that became a region of China (called Inner Mongolia). As the Soviet Union began to break up in the early 1990s, many aspects of traditional Mongolian culture slowly returned. In the last few years, the Mongolian government has started teaching the traditional script in schools.

Mongolian script is slowly being revived today.

not interested in novels. They preferred poetry and essays, and these two written forms did not receive as much support from the Mongols as plays and novels. Chinese poetry and essays were steeped in conventions that were hundreds of years old by the time the Mongols arrived in China, and embodied Confucian ideals with which educated Chinese were familiar. For the Mongols, however, these very formal, subtle forms of literature were not as interesting or meaningful as the more narrative plays and novels. Still, Khubilai and his successors did invite poets to their palaces.

The Visual Arts in Mongol China

Khubilai and the other Mongol rulers of China appreciated their subjects' skills in the visual arts. The Chinese had a long history as talented painters, sculptors, and porcelain makers. They carved intricate designs into ivory, jade, and lacquer, a hard material made from the sap of Asian trees. Chinese artisans also produced colorful textiles out of silk and cotton. Some of these textiles were worn as clothes, while others were hung on walls as art.

The Mongols did not make any specific contributions to the visual arts in China, but several noticeable developments occurred under their rule. Some of the educated Confucians who were kept out of government service turned to the arts for work and self-expression. Under the Yuan, a style of painting called *wen ren hua* first appeared. The name means "literary man's painting" in Chinese; the works were painted by well-educated amateur artists and were intended to appeal to the educated. *Wen ren hua* artists often painted highly detailed scenes from nature that depicted their own emotions. Their work differed from the paintings done by "official" artists, who had trained at the Song academy for art. Traditional paintings focused on portraits, religious subjects, and scenes from everyday life. One Chinese painter at the Great Khan's court, Zhao Mengfu (1254–1322), was famous for his paintings of horses, a popular subject with the Mongols.

Sculpture under the Mongols tended to focus on traditional subjects. Most sculptures were made for Buddhist patrons and focused on religious subjects. Sculptors worked with stone, wood, and bronze to create their images. Artists also carved reliefs–three-dimensional images that rose out from a flat surface.

Under Khubilai, northern and southern Chinese artistic styles came together. His rule also helped bring Chinese influences to other lands, such as Persia, and introduced foreign artistic elements to China. One important influence came to the empire from Tibet. Aniga (1244–1306), a Tibetan Buddhist artist and architect originally from Nepal, impressed the Phags-pa Lama with his artistic talents. The lama brought the artist to Khubilai, who commissioned him to build temples and other buildings in Shangdu and Khan-baliq. Aniga also designed gold jewelry, and the Great Khan eventually had him supervise all the artisans in China. The Tibetan influence on Chinese art included the depiction of religious figures wearing jewelry and colorful ornaments.

Science and Technology in Mongol China

The geographic range of the Mongol Empire helped bring new ideas to China. At the same time, the Mongols took Chinese technology and spread it to western Asia. One important Chinese technology was printing. The Chinese published the first books by carving characters onto wooden blocks. After dipping each block in ink, the printer pressed it onto a page. Block printing was used in China for centuries, and historian Paul D. Buell suggests that the Mongols might have taken this process to the Mid-

A NEW KIND OF CERAMICS

One artistic innovation during Yuan times was the appearance of blue-and-white porcelain. This development did not occur with direct royal support, though in general the potters of the empire had great freedom to create what they wanted. The distinct blue-and-white style remained popular in China for several hundred years, and is often associated with the later Ming Dynasty.

dle East. As noted earlier in this chapter, Khubilai encouraged printing in China, which helped spread literacy there in the dynasties that followed the Yuan.

For many of his personal and political decisions, Khubilai relied on astrology. He and other Mongols wanted to know what might happen in the future, to help them make decisions. Marco Polo noted (in *The Travels of Marco Polo*) that the capital city of Khan-baliq had "about five thousand astrologers and soothsayers" who "predict that there shall be thunder and storm in a certain month, earthquakes in another . . . " To help his astrologers, Khubilai built a large observatory in Khan-baliq, where astronomers calculated the positions of the stars and planets. These people combined real science with astrology in their work. Many of the most learned astrologer/astronomers were Persian. The Chinese astronomer Guo Shoujing (1232–1316) used a Persian calendar as the basis for his own accurate calendar.

After their conquests, the Mongols turned to outsiders for new medical knowledge. During their early nomadic years, the Mongols relied mostly on their shamans to heal them using herbal remedies and by making contact with the spirit world. Their exposure to more scientific approaches to healing came from the Chinese and Tibetan Buddhists and the Persian Muslims. Khubilai built a large medical college that housed ancient Chinese medical texts written on stone slabs.

Chinese medicine was based on the idea that the body is filled with a special energy called *qi*. Blocked or unbalanced *qi* leads to illness, and doctors use herbal medicine and acupuncture to try to restore the correct flow and balance of the energy. With acupuncture, the doctors place very thin needles

Why Is It So Hard to Make a Calendar?

Early peoples marked the months by the phases of the moon and the years by the movements of the sun and the change of seasons. Since the 12 phases of the moon add up to only about 354 days, while the year lasts about 365 1/4 days, the phases of the moon, movements of the sun, and change of seasons rapidly get out of sync.

Different cultures have solved this problem in different ways. In ancient Rome, Julius Caesar followed the advice of Egyptian astronomers and designed a calendar that ignored the phases of the moon and only followed the sun. This Julian calendar is the ancestor of the Gregorian calendar used today in most of the world. Muslims use a lunar calendar that follows only the moon and ignores the sun. Thus, the new year slowly cycles through all four seasons.

The Chinese calendar followed both the moon and the sun, but used a complex mathematical formula to add in extra months every few years to balance the two. The Mongols also adopted this system.

at specific spots on a patient's body. Chinese doctors also use acupuncture on animals. A document from just after the end of the Yuan Dynasty shows where acupuncture needles should be placed to cure a horse's ailments. Persian influence gave Chinese doctors new herbal drugs, and a Muslim medical book discussed how to treat burns, animal bites, and other wounds. The exchange also went the other way, as Hülegü seems to have brought some Chinese medical practices to Persia.

For the Mongols, the influence of Persian and Chinese technology was greatest in warfare. Historians are not sure where gunpowder was first used in warfare, although they know the Chinese used it to make fireworks around 1000. The Chinese also used it in grenades, but they may have learned how to make these small explosives from the Muslims of Syria. In addition, the Chinese had simple guns that fired arrows. The Mongols used all these weapons, and they may have been the first people to use cannons, designed by their Chinese engineers.

The Song seem to have developed the first land mines in their efforts to stop the Mongol invasion. With one type, an enemy was lured to the mine with some kind of desirable object, such as an abandoned weapon. As the soldier neared the lure, he stepped on a device just under the ground that lit a fuse and exploded gunpowder. Under Mongol rule, Chinese engineers also developed naval mines. A bomb was placed in an inflated animal skin, and an incense stick served as the fuse. The bomb floated on the water near an enemy ship until the incense stick burned down and set off the gunpowder.

From the Persians, the Mongols in China borrowed the design for catapults, which could hurl either large stones or exploding bombs. The Chinese referred to one kind of catapult as the "Muslim engine." Marco Polo claims he showed the Mongols how to build a kind of catapult called a trebuchet, but these machines were already being used before he reached China. These catapults used a system of weights to lengthen or shorten the range of the missile being fired.

Persian Culture and the Mongols

As in China, when the Mongols invaded Persia they found a country with a long and rich cultural history. At its peak around 500 B.C.E., the Persian Empire reached from the Oxus River to northern Egypt, and it absorbed the art and technology of ancient civilizations, such as Egypt, Babylonia, and Assyria. After the Persian Empire began to weaken, it came under the influence of ancient Greece and Rome. The last major cultural influence on

CONNECTIONS >>>>>>>>>>>>

Hot-Air Balloons

The Mongols borrowed another military idea from the Chinese and brought it with them on their European invasion of 1241. The Chinese developed the first simple hot-air balloons. At Liegnitz, in Poland, the Mongols used one shaped like a dragon as a signal for their troops. Later, European scientists began exploring the idea of using hot gases to lift humans off the ground. The first balloon flight with a human onboard took place in France in 1783. Today hot-air balloonists still rise above the ground for races, long-distance travel, and short rides over beautiful countryside.

the region was Islam, which reached Persia soon after it was founded in the seventh century.

The rulers of Persia before the Mongols were the Seljuks, a nomadic Turkic people who had converted to Islam. Under their rule, both Arabic—the language of Islam in religious affairs—and Persian were used. Eventually Persian became the official language of the state, and since the Mongol Ilkhans relied on Persian officials to run the government, Persian remained the major everyday language. According to modern scholar Abolala Soudavar (writing in *The Court of the Il-Khans, 1290-1340*) Persian officials in the Mongol government also "were able to lure Mongol royalty . . . into the wonderful world of Persian literature and culture."

The Written Arts in the Ilkhanate

Persia had many great poets in its long history. Under the Seljuks, some poets wrote book-length works on personal subjects, while others wrote poems praising their rulers. During the first decades of the Mongol conquest, however, poetry declined in Persia. Many poets and other artists either died during the invasions or fled to other countries. Under Mongol rule, poetry never regained the prominence it once had. The city of Shiraz, however, escaped Mongol destruction, and it produced several notable poets. One of these was Sadi (c. 1184–1291), who followed a branch of Islam called Sufism. Sufis believe a person must go beyond the rules and regulations of religious life and search for a direct experience of God. Sadi's most famous work, the *Gulistan* (Rose Garden), uses poetry and short sayings to instruct others—especially rulers—on how to live a good and meaningful life. He wrote (quoted in http://classics.mit.edu/Sadi/gulistan.2.i.html), "All this is nothing as it passes away: Throne and luck, command and prohibition, taking and giving." Power and riches, the poet meant, did not last forever, and were not important to living a spiritual life.

Although poetry struggled under the Mongols, another form of literature reached its peak. Historiography is the study of history using different original sources over time, trying to show how earlier historians may have distorted facts or made errors. It is the history of the history of a particular subject, and requires a historian to carefully weigh other historians' methods and prejudices. Under the Mongols, Persian scholars excelled at historiography and general history. Writing in *The Cambridge History of Iran*, J. Rypka says, " . . . the principal historical works of the Mongol period are amongst the finest ever produced by any of the Islamic people."

The historical writing of the Ilkhanate rested on several key factors. For one, the Mongols believed they were on a divine mission to rule the world, and they wanted their reign well documented. The Persians also had access to documents from all across the Mongol Empire, and some historians lived through the events they described, so they were able to add descriptions and quotes from their direct knowledge. At their best, the Persians wrote history with the flair of good literature.

The first of the great Persian historians under the Mongols was Juvaini (1226–1283). He worked for the Mongol government, serving in Baghdad. His greatest work was the three-volume *History of the World Conqueror*, about Chinggis and the Mongol Empire until 1258. The first volume detailed Chinggis's rise to power and included the brief rule of his son Küyük. The second focused on Khorazm and Persia and the Mongol presence there, while the last dealt with Möngke Khan's reign in the 1250s.

Even more notable was Rashid al-Din (1247–1318). Like Juvaini, he served as a Mongol official as well as a historian. Originally trained as a doctor, Rashid al-Din worked for the Ilkhan Ghazan, who asked him to write a history of the Mongols in Persia. The scholar went beyond that, writing a multi-volume work that also included a history of Mongol China and Europe.

A Sufi Who Fled

The first Mongol conquest under Chinggis dramatically changed the life of another Sufi poet. Jalal al-Din Rumi (1207–1273) was born on the eastern edge of the Persia, in what is now Afghanistan. When the Mongols roared through that region around 1221, Rumi fled to Syria and then settled in what is now Turkey. During his travels, he met religious figures who shaped his beliefs, and those beliefs influenced his art. Rumi not only wrote poetry, he also developed a type of spinning dance that leads to a form of religious meditation. Some Sufis, known as "whirling dervishes," still do this dance. Rumi's poetry was largely unknown in the Western world until relatively recently. Now he is often read and quoted by people who follow spiritual paths that stress love and tolerance for all people, as the poet did.

Burial Monument
The tomb of Ulijaytu Khodabendeh still stands in Sultaniyya, Iran, a testament to to the lavish tombs wealthy Mongols of the Ilkhanate built for themselves.

Persian Visual Arts

In arts and crafts, the Persians continued many old Seljuk styles during the Mongols' rule. In ceramics and other crafts, certain images were commonly used through the end of the 13th century. These included representations of stars and planets and people performing everyday activities. Craftsmen also illustrated scenes from the *Shah-nama* (Book of Kings), a poetic history of Persia's rulers.

Centuries after the Mongols lost control in Persia, Iranian scholars wrote that painting truly blossomed under their rule. Rashid al-Din started a school for artists, and Ghazan and the Ilkhans who followed him supported the arts. Painting received a boost when the Ilkhans commissioned an epic history of their rule, similar to the *Shah-nama*. The Mongols had Persian artists illustrate scenes from the history, and illustrated books became a long-lasting art form in Persia. Illustrating the books required small, detailed paintings, called miniatures, and some Chinese artistic styles were included in these works. The Chinese influence can be seen in how mountains and people are drawn. The Persian artists, however, were the true masters of miniature painting.

Rashid al-Din also played a role in the building projects of the Mongol era. Persian architecture reflected styles that existed throughout the Islamic world, with domed buildings that had as many as 12 walls. The wealthy Persians and Mongols of the Ilkhanate spent lavishly on large burial complexes. For the Mongols, building public tombs was a break from tradition. In their nomadic past, Mongol rulers always had themselves buried in secret locations. With their conversion to Islam, the Ilkhans followed the example of earlier Persian rulers. Ghazan, for example, built a 12-sided tomb surrounded by a mosque, schools, and a hospital. The complex also featured a pool house and a fountain. Later rulers of Persia and neighboring lands, such as the Ottoman Turks, copied the Mongol style in burial sites.

In Sultaniyya, the Ilkhan Öljeitü built himself a large tomb complex, or mausoleum. This domed mausoleum has been called one of the greatest construction projects carried out by a Mongol ruler. Part of the mausoleum still stands in Sultaniyya, where it is a popular tourist attraction.

Persian Science

As noted earlier in this chapter, Khubilai Khan brought Persian astronomers to China. Islamic scholars were known for their scientific and mathematical pursuits. Persia and other lands of the Middle East benefited from their exposure to both Western and Indian scientific traditions. Mathematics was used to calculate the position of stars and planets, helping to create accurate calendars. Modern algebra is based on work done by Islamic scholars, and the word *algebra* comes from the Arabic word *al-jabr*, which means the joining together of disorganized parts.

Under the Mongols, Persian mathematicians mostly improved on work that had been done a few centuries earlier, rather than making new discoveries. In astronomy, however, scientists under the Mongols excelled. The first Persian to work for the Mongols was Nasir al-Din (1200–1273). Hülegü built an observatory for him at Maragha, in what is now northwest Iran. It has been called the world's first true observatory for studying the skies. Nasir al-Din and other astronomers studied the orbits of the planets.

A scientist named Kamal al-Din (d. c. 1320) studied at the Maragha observatory, but he focused more on optics and light than on the stars and planets. He wanted to understand why humans saw rainbows. With his experiments, he learned that light passing through water at a certain angle creates the colors that make up a rainbow.

JUDGING THE HISTORIANS

Modern-day readers of Juvaini and Rashid al-Din must do their own historiographical examinations. Both men tried to be fair and accurate. Still, they were employed by the Mongols and could not be overly critical of them, which may have influenced what they wrote. Rashid al-Din in particular wanted to show that the Mongol rulers before Ghazan had harmed Persia, while Ghazan's reforms were helpful.

Art and Culture in Mongol Russia

The khans of the Golden Horde did not inherit the same rich cultures that existed in China and Persia. In many ways, they remained truer to their native Mongol culture. Still, historians believe they did promote some arts and sciences, though the historical evidence is weak.

In Russia, major support for the arts came from the Russian Orthodox Church. The Mongol policy of religious tolerance helped the church thrive, and it was able to build churches and commission religious artwork. The most common form of art was the icon, a painting on wood of saints and other holy figures. People kept icons in their homes and considered them holy objects. Icons were powerful symbols of the importance of the Christian faith, especially among uneducated peasants who could not read the Bible. Although icon painting developed centuries earlier in the Byzantine Empire, icons became more common during the Mongol era, especially in the cities of Novgorod and Moscow. During the first years of Mongol conquest, icon painting suffered. When the Mongols ended their attacks and simply collected tribute, the art form regained strength.

The Russian Orthodox Church also shaped musical development in Russia. The introduction of Christianity brought chanting, a form of sung prayer. The Russians combined Byzantine chanting traditions with their own folk songs, creating what was called *znamenny* chant. This musical form survived through the Mongol era, although written records of the chants did not.

Russian literature during the Mongol period was mostly limited to chronicles. These recorded historical events of the city-states that emerged before and during the Golden Horde's rule. But the chronicles also had elements of myth or fable, so they cannot always be trusted as true history. Most of the chronicles focused on religious and political events and ideas, trying to build pride in the Orthodox Church and local leaders. The Mongols, not surprisingly, begin to appear in the chronicles after the first Mongol invasions, though at times the authors

CONNECTIONS >>>>>>>>>>>

Chant Today

In recent decades, some Western music fans have become interested in the religious chants of medieval times, recorded by modern singers. Although *znamenny* chant eventually lost popularity among most Russians, some featuring traditional Orthodox Church music have been recorded on CDs. Orthodox chant has also inspired a number of modern composers, including John Tavener (b. 1944). A British composer who was received into the Russian Orthodox Church in 1977, he studied *znamenny* chant and uses elements of it in his music.

seem to ignore Mongol rule. The first mention of the "Tatars" in the chronicles from Novgorod says, " . . . no one knew who they were or where the came from. . . . Today they come to take our land, and they will come to take yours tomorrow" (as quoted in Charles J. Halperin's *The Tatar Yoke*).

The Cultural World of the Ulus Chaghatai

As in the lands of the Golden Horde, the rulers of the Ulus Chaghatai largely remained true to their Mongol cultural roots. In Central Asia, the Mongols found a culture influenced by Turkic. Persian, and Arab sources. The Mongols avoided the region's large cities, where art and culture—influenced by Islam—had flourished for several centuries.

The sedentary areas that survived the Mongol invasion did not see many changes. The cities of Transoxiana continued to educate their children and support artisans. During the 12th century, the region had produced one of the greatest medieval doctors, known in Europe as Avicenna (980–1037). His medical books were read throughout the Middle East and parts of Christian lands. Other notable books from the pre-Mongol period included a dictionary of Turkic phrases.

The Ulus Chaghatai saw a great period of artistic expression under the Timurids, the rulers who followed Tamerlane (see chapter 3). The Timurids turned away from conquest and focused on large building projects, mostly in Samarkand. On the walls of some buildings were elaborate mosaics.

The greatest Timurid patron of art and science may have been Ulugh Beg (1394–1449), a grandson of Tamerlane. On the wall of one school he built (according to Svat Soucek in *A History of Inner Asia*) were the words "The search for knowledge is every Muslim's duty." The astronomers he gathered created detailed charts of the stars that corrected mistakes from earlier works. The ruler himself took part in some of this work, and he also found time to write poetry and compose music. His brother Baysunghur (1397–1433) had a similar influence on Central Asian culture in Herat, in what is now Afghanistan.

Despite their reputation as violent barbarians, the various branches of Chinggis's family played a role in keeping the arts and sciences alive for several centuries. The great cultures of Persia and China continued to thrive, and ideas shared across Mongol lands influenced old ways of thinking and creating art.

Epilogue

THE WEAKENING AND EVENTUAL COLLAPSE OF THE TIMURID Dynasty was not the end of Mongol involvement in Central Asian politics. Several more dynasties with family ties to Chinggis Khan emerged, though a 13th-century Mongol would have little in common with these later Mongols. Most of the new rulers spoke Turkic, practiced Islam, and knew Persian culture; the Mongol language and culture were limited to the traditional homelands and lands bordering them.

The people with Mongol ties included the Uzbeks, who developed in an *ulus* that once belonged to Chinggis's grandson Shiban (dates unknown). This land near the Ural Mountains bordered the Russian holdings of the Golden Horde. During the 1430s, the Uzbeks moved close to Transoxiana, and during the early 1500s their ruler Muhammad Shibani (1451–1510) took control of Timurid lands. A true descendant of Chinggis now ruled a large part of what had been the Ulus Chaghatai. The last great dynasty with ties to Chinggis, however, reached its peak in lands outside the traditional Mongol empire.

The Mughals of India

The eastern half of Chaghatai's old realm had been called Moghulistan since the mid 14th century (see chapter 3). The people who lived there were called Moghuls or Chaghatais. In English, *Moghul* is sometimes written *Mughal*, and that name is used for a dynasty that ruled in northern India for almost four centuries.

The founder of this dynasty was Zahirrudin Babur (1483–1530), a Timurid who also had family ties to Chinggis. From his base in Fergana, a region in what is now Uzbekistan, he wanted to reestablish Tamerlane's old

Many Names

Around 1460, a group of rebel Uzbeks left their ruler and joined up with nomads from what had been the Blue Horde of Kazakhstan. Together they formed a small khanate and were called Kazakhs. In later centuries, Russians gave them a new name, calling them Kyrgyz (also spelled Kirghiz). Today, both names can be seen in the geography of Central Asia, in the nations of Kazakhstan and Kyrgyzstan. Both countries have a population that combines descendants of the Turko-Mongols with ethnic Russians.

empire. The Uzbeks and the Persians, however, controlled most of those lands at the beginning of the 16th century, so Babur decided instead to invade northern India (sometimes called Hindustan), just as Tamerlane had. After his victories, Babur used his ancestor's previous conquests to justify his rule.

Babur's Mughal Dynasty thrived, thanks to the gold and silver of northern India. His successor created an empire that covered two-thirds of modern India, as well as parts of Pakistan and Afghanistan. Through the 17th century, the Mughal leaders considered themselves Central Asians, not Indians. They treasured their ties to Tamerlane, and the first rulers of the dynasty honored their Mongol heritage. They often noted in official records that they followed the rules and customs of Chinggis Khan.

The Russian Empire

The Mughals built one of the world's greatest empires. Some of their kings dreamed of winning back their ancestors' homelands in Central Asia, but they never fulfilled that dream. But a later empire did span the lands of the old Ulus Chaghatai, and included the former Golden Horde and part of the Ilkhanate as well. With the end of Mongol control in Russia, the princes of Moscow rose to create the modern state of Russia. The czars, as the Russian emperors were later called, then expanded into Central Asia. Many of the Mongols' former lands were ruled by Europeans for the first time. The Russians, however, were not typical Europeans because their culture and politics had been shaped by Mongol rule the 13th and 14th centuries. Among medieval Europeans, only the Slavic Russians had been dominated by a nomadic people from Central Asia.

By the 17th century, Russia's czars were moving eastward across the northern tier of Eurasia. They had already defeated the remnants of the Golden Horde, except the Crimean Tatars. During the 18th century, Russia moved into the steppes of Central Asia, the heart of what had been the

Mongol Empire. Turko-Mongol traders worked with Russian merchants, and khans of small Tatar hordes declared their loyalty to the czars. Where they could not take over peacefully, the Russians used superior military force to take control of former Mongol lands. By the end of the 18th century, Russia had built its own empire in Central Asia. According to historian Hidehiro Okada, writing in *The Mongol Empire and Its Legacy*, the Russians had an easier time asserting their rule because of the example set by Chinggis hundreds of years before. The Great Khan claimed he had a god-given right to unify the world; the idea of a single powerful state across Central Asia endured long after Chinggis was gone.

The Russian presence brought peace to a region that often saw local rivalries lead to war. The Russians also brought modern European technology to the nomadic lands, building the first railroads and telegraph lines. Czarist rule in Central Asia also led many Russians and Ukrainians to set-

The Last of the Mongols
The Crimean Tatars were the last of the Golden Horde in Russia. This French engraving from 1888 shows the interior of a Crimean Tatar tent.

tle in the region, spreading both the Russian language and Orthodox Christianity to new regions. Still, Islam and traditional languages continued to thrive. But along with the benefits of Russian rule came policies that were as bad as the worst of Mongol dominance in Russia. The czars imposed heavy taxes and forced civilians into military service. They also supported serfdom, a system similar to slavery that forced peasants to work for wealthy landowners. Serfs had some legal protections, but they could not leave their masters' lands. Russian serfdom did not end until 1861. (Serfdom, however, was never applied in Siberia or Central Asia.)

Russia's eastward movement across Asia brought it into direct contact with both China and Mongolia. By the 19th century China was ruled by the Qing Dynasty. As the Russians had done, the Qing

Foreign Domination

Two Mongolian men walk past a wall showing photographs of all the Communist leaders in their region, Uliastay. This photo was taken in 1984, when Mongolia was completely dominated by the Soviet Union.

emperors claimed a right to rule all the lands around them, because of their historical link to the Yuan Dynasty of the Mongols. China took control of Mongolia in 1691, although the Mongol homeland remained under the control of local nobles descended from Chinggis Khan. It was known as Outer Mongolia, to distinguish it from Inner Mongolia, a part of the old Mongol homelands whose Mongol nobles were tightly controlled by the Qing Emperors.

Modern Mongolia

In 1917, Russian revolutionaries overthrew their country's last czar and eventually installed a communist government. Under communism, the state owns almost all property, and one political party—the Communist Party—controls the government and the economy. The Russian Communists divided the vast territory they controlled into a series of republics and called them the Union of Soviet Socialist Republics. Moscow was the capital of this new nation, and Russia was the dominant republic. The Soviet Union created 14 other Soviet Socialist Republics, and most had once been part of the Mongol Empire. These territories were centered in what had been the Ulus Chaghatai, the northeastern part of the Ilkhanate, and the southern and eastern lands of the Golden Horde. The five in Central Asia were Kazakhstan, Uzbekistan, Kyrgyzstan, Tajikistan, and Turkmenistan. Georgia, Armenia, and Azerbaijan were under Ilkhanate influence, while the Golden Horde ruled or influenced what became Russia, Belarus, Moldova, and Ukraine. (After the collapse of the Soviet Union at the end of 1991, all these republics became independent nations.)

In 1921 Soviet troops helped the Mongolians in Outer Mongolia defeat Chinese forces and Russians who opposed communism. In 1924, Mongolia declared its independence as the People's Republic of Mongolia, though in reality it came under the direct influence of the Soviet Union. Some Mongols also lived in lands that were part of Soviet Union.

Under Soviet domination, Mongolia adopted a Communist government. As in the Soviet Union, members of the Communist Party dominated all aspects of politics and the economy. Officials cracked down on the Mongolians' traditional religions—Buddhism and shamanism. The Communists destroyed temples and killed monks. The Soviets forced the Mongolians to abandon their traditional writing system and use the Russian alphabet.

The Soviet influence, however, also led to some positive change, as education spread and farming methods improved. Still, the Mongols lacked political and cultural freedom. They also became extremely isolated from the rest of the world; the Soviets set up military bases across Mongolia and pressured the country to forbid tourism in order to maintain secrecy at these bases. But Mongolia threw off its ties to Soviets in 1991, and Mongolian leaders began creating democratic political systems.

In 1990, when Mongolians began demanding changes in their government, some protesters carried signs saying *morindoo*—"mount up." This was the cry Chinggis Khan used to send

CONNECTIONS >>>>>>>>>>>>

Unrest in Inner Mongolia

More Mongolians live in China than in Mongolia. Inner Mongolia, still a part of China, runs along the southern and eastern border of Mongolia and China. It includes large stretches of the Gobi Desert. China named Inner Mongolia an "autonomous region" in 1947, which in theory means the people there govern themselves. In reality, the Chinese are firmly in control. Chinese immigrants began ploughing up the Mongol steppes and pastures on a large scale in the early 1900s. And since 1947, the Chinese have established vast mines, steel mills, and cashmere mills to exploit Inner Mongolia's resources. Over the past few decades the Chinese have tried to weaken Mongol culture by sending ethnic Chinese to work and live in Inner Mongolia; ethnic Chinese now outnumber the Mongols by about six to one. Since the 1990s, some Mongols have protested the Chinese assault on their culture and limits on their political freedom.

CONNECTIONS >>>>>>>>>>>>

The Tatars Today

The Russians called the Mongols of the Golden Horde *Tatars*, taking the name from one of the tribes Chinggis Khan had defeated when he unified Mongolia. From this name, Europeans came up with *Tartars*. Some historical sources claim this name was a reference to Greek mythology: Tartarus was the deepest part of hell, where wicked people received their punishment after they died. To the Europeans, the Mongols seemed as if they were demons from hell, so it made sense to change their name from *Tatars* to *Tartars*.

During World War II, Soviet leader Joseph Stalin forced the remaining Tatars of the Crimea to leave their homes and settle in other regions of the Soviet Union—a country which included Russia and other Central Asian lands. He feared the Tatars would help the Germans in their fight against the Soviet Union. Today, thousands of Crimean Tatars are still trying to return to their homeland, which is now part of Ukraine. Descendants of the Golden Horde also live today in Tatarstan.

his troops into battle. Today, the Mongols try to balance their nomadic ways from the past with modern life. People still live in felt *gers*, but outside the tent a solar-powered satellite dish pulls in television signals from around the world. Young boys still learn to ride bareback on horses, then perhaps grow up to attend college and study engineering. Journalist Glenn Hodges, in an article published in the October 2003 issue of *National Geographic*, quotes Mongolian prime minister Nambaryn Enkhbayar, "In order to survive we have to stop being nomads." Yet many Mongols still choose the nomadic life–their main tie to the past glory of Chinggis Khan.

The Mongol Legacy

Unlike the Romans and their Latin language, the Mongols did not give their subjects a new universal tongue. Unlike the British, who brought democratic forms of government to new lands, the Mongols did not leave a new, lasting political legacy across their empire. But the Mongol invasions influenced Asia and Europe in many ways.

Thanks to the Mongols, the Ming Dynasty ruled a united China, and that unity remains today. China under the Mongols also made greater contact with the outside world than at any other time in its prior history. The Mongol presence in Russia, through the Golden Horde, helped the princes of Moscow gain power and eventually build their own Central Asian empire. In Persia, the Ilkhans promoted the arts and helped the Persian language thrive, replacing Arabic as the main language. The Mongols' religious tolerance also saw Roman Catholicism make its first gains in East Asia, and Buddhism spread into new areas. The Mongols also welcomed Islam and boosted its presence throughout Central Asia.

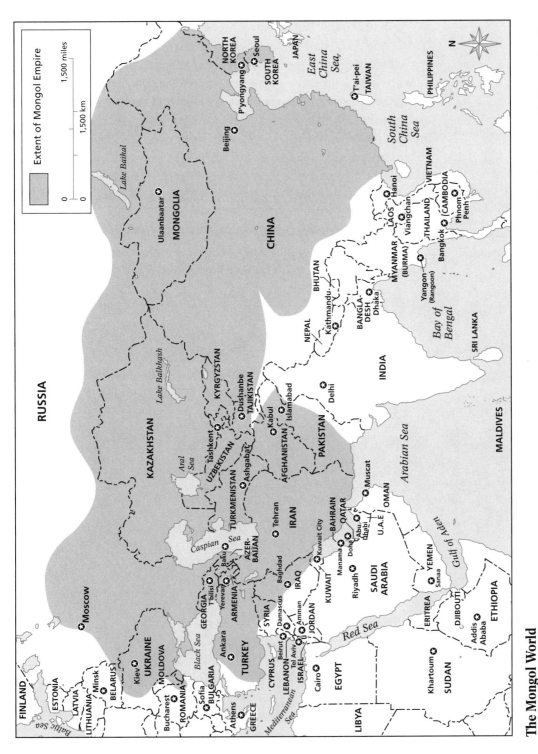

The Mongol World
Mongol influence stretched from from Korea to Eastern Europe and constituted the largest continuous area of land ever controlled by one family.

Another important feature of Mongol rule was greater contact between Europe and Asia. That contact, helped by the writings of several European priests and explorers, eventually led the nations of Europe to seek sea routes to Asia. By sea, the Europeans could trade directly for the highly valued spices of the Far East, instead of dealing with Central Asian and Middle Eastern merchants who controlled the land trade with eastern Asia. The desire for a new sea route to Asia inspired Christopher Columbus to travel west instead of east, as the sailors before him did. His voyages led Europeans to discover the "New Worlds" of North and South America. And perhaps the Mongols would have had an even greater impact on Europe if the death of their leader had not stopped their march into Europe during the 13th century. The Europeans of that era were barely prepared to fight such a superior force.

After the Mongols, no other nomadic people from the steppes challenged the power of sedentary societies. Modern technology changed

Old and New

This photo was taken in 2004 just outside the Mongolian capital of Ulaanbaatar. Many Mongolian farmers and herders still live in gers—with television sets.

CONNECTIONS >>>>>>>>>>>>>>

The Lasting Attraction of Chinggis Khan

Today, the first Great Khan is honored across Mongolia. While some Asians and Europeans remember him as a bloodthirsty conqueror, modern Mongolians see him a strong leader who united their people and created an empire that still shapes life in Eurasia. In 1962, the Mongolian government erected a statue of Chinggis Khan in honor of his 800th birthday. He is a visible source of pride for most Mongolians. His name has also appeared on products, such as Genghis Khan vodka, and his face has appeared on Mongolia's money.

Chinggis/Genghis Khan also appeals to Western filmmakers. In 2004, action film star Steven Seagal traveled to China to begin making a movie about the first Great Khan. Seagal planned to play the title role. This movie comes almost 50 years after the famous American actor John Wayne played Chinggis in a movie called *The Conqueror*.

warfare. Archers shooting from horseback could not compete with heavy artillery. And once the nomads stopped raiding others for their wealth, they could not compete with the growing economies of the cities of Eurasia. Even in their own homeland, until just recently, the Mongols had to accept foreign domination.

Historians David O. Morgan and Reuven Amitai-Preiss, in the introduction to *The Mongol Empire and Its Legacy*, say the Mongols benefited from "the medieval equivalent of public relations consultants." Such writers as Marco Polo and Rashid al-Din painted colorful, detailed portraits of the Mongols and their khanates. Thanks to those works, Morgan and Amitai-Preiss say, "the Mongols have remained on center-stage in the human imagination for hundreds of years." The Mongols still amaze because no other people ever built such a massive empire so quickly. They fascinate because they mixed horrible cruelties with wise policies. And in parts of the world, the Mongol impact is still felt today.

TIME LINE

1206	The Mongols elect Temüjin as their leader, and he takes the name Chinggis Khan.
1209	Chinggis leads his first foreign invasions, against the Tanguts of Xixia.
1218	The Mongols launch their first major attack in the West, invading Khorazm.
1227	Chinggis Khan dies.
1229	Chinggis's son Ögedei is named the new Great Khan.
1234	The Mongols defeat the Jin Empire of northern China.
1237–1240	The Mongols establish control over northwest Russia, which is later known as the Kipchak Khanate or Golden Horde.
1242	The western campaign in Europe ends after the death of Ögedei.
1256	Hülegü begins the Mongol conquest of Persia, leading to the creation of the Ilkhanate.
1260	Khubilai Khan is chosen as the fifth Great Khan. A defeat in Syria ends the Mongols' westward drive across the Middle East.
1271	Khubilai Khan claims the title of emperor of China and founds the Yuan Dynasty.
1279	Khubilai Khan defeats the Song and reunites northern and southern China.
1294	Khubilai Khan dies. His grandson Tëmur Öljeitü becomes the Great Khan.
1295	The Ilkhan Ghazan converts to Islam.
1334	The Ulus Chaghatai begins to split in half.
1335	Abu Said, the last Ilkhan, dies. The Ilkhanate breaks up.
1360	The Golden Horde breaks up.
1368	The Yuan Dynasty is replaced by the Ming Dynasty, ending Mongol rule in China.
1370	Tamerlane rises to power in the Ulus Chaghatai.
1380	Russians defeat the Golden Horde at Kulikovo Pole.
1395	Tamerlane defeats Toqtamish, severely weakening the Golden Horde's rule in Russia.
1405	Tamerlane dies before his planned invasion of China.
1480	Ivan the Great of Moscow defies the Golden Horde.
1504	Babur, a descendant of Tamerlane and Chinggis, begins the conquests that lead to the founding of the Mughal Empire of India.

RESOURCES: Books

Atwood, Christopher. *Encyclopedia of Mongolia and the Mongol Empire* (New York: Facts On File, 2004)
   This book offers a comprehensive look at the nation of Mongolia, past and present.

Martell, Hazel Mary. *The World of Islam Before 1700* (Austin, Tex.: Raintree Steck-Vaughn, 1998)
   Islam was the dominant faith in much of the Mongol Empire. This book traces the development of Islam from the seventh century until after the end of the Mongol era.

Nicolle, David. *The Mongol Warlords* (Dorset, England: Firebird Books, 1990)
   A look at four major Mongol rulers and their tactics on the battlefield. Many full-page color illustrations provide a vivid look at life during Mongol times.

Pang, Guek-Cheng. *Mongolia* (New York: Marshall Cavendish, 2000)
   Traces the history of Mongolia with an emphasis on modern-day life in that country. The book examines such topics as religion, art, languages, and festivals.

Polo, Marco. *The Travels of Marco Polo*, Translated by William Marsden, edited by Manuel Komroff (New York: The Modern Library, 2001)
   An easy-to-read version of the classic that describes Marco Polo's observations of the Mongol Empire. The editor includes footnotes to help explain some of the text.

Stewart, Stanley. *In the Empire of Genghis Khan: A Journey Among Nomads* (Guilford, Conn.: The Lyons Press, 2002)
   Stanley Stewart, a journalist, retraces the route of William of Rubruck, a 13th-century monk who visited Mongolia. The book draws parallels between Mongol life in that era and modern times.

Taylor, Robert. *Life in Genghis Khan's Mongolia* (San Diego, Calif.: Lucent Books, 2001)
   This book covers Chinggis's rise to power, as well as social life within the empire he created. Boxes deal with such issues as women wrestlers and Mongol personal habits.

Worth, Richard. *The Great Empire of China and Marco Polo in World History* (Berkeley Heights, N.J.: Enslow Publishers, 2003)
   This book describes China during the reign of Khubilai Khan, focusing on the travels of Marco Polo. The author also addresses the historical debate regarding the truth of Polo's claims.

RESOURCES: Web Sites

Modern Mongolia: Reclaiming Genghis Khan
www.museum.upenn.edu/Mongolia/index.shtml
> The web site has a history of Mongolia from ancient times to today, and a detailed look at modern Mongolia's links to its past. A companion site to an exhibit created by the University of Pennsylvania Museum of Archaeology and Anthropology.

Mongol-American Cultural Association
www.maca-usa.org/pages/1/index.htm
> The web site for this group explains ways in which traditional Mongol culture endures in the United States. The group holds an annual Chinggis Khan celebration, and the web site includes photos from this event.

Mongol Art
www.mongolart.mn
> The Arts Council of Mongolia sponsors this site, which traces the history of many art forms in Mongolia. Current artwork is also featured.

Pre-Modern Imperialism: The Mongols
www.accd.edu/sac/history/keller/Mongols/intro.html
> This site covers both the main Mongol Empire and the smaller empires that developed after it. It offers detailed looks at Chinggis Khan and the Mongol army, as well as a time line.

The Silk Road Foundation
www.silk-road.com/toc/index.html
> This group, dedicated to the study of the Silk Road and Central Asia, offers information on the Mongols and other people who ruled this region. The site includes maps of the Mongol Empire and major trade routes in Central Asia.

The Silver Horde
SilverHorde.viahistoria.com/main.html
> This web site features the activities of Mongol reenactors—people who dress up as Mongols and try to duplicate Mongol culture, especially military life. The site has detailed information on Mongol military practices.

BIBLIOGRAPHY

Amitai-Preiss, Reuven, and David O. Morgan, Ed., *The Mongol Empire and its Legacy*. Leiden, Netherlands: Brille, 1999.

Barraclough, Geoffrey, Ed., *The Times Concise Atlas of World History*. Maplewood, N.J.: Hammond Inc., 1982.

Bingham, Woodbridge, Hilary Conroy, and Frank W. Iklé, *A History of Asia*, Volume 1. Boston: Allyn and Bacon, 1974.

Boyle, J.A., Ed., *The Cambridge History of Iran,* Volume 5: The Saljuq and Mongol Periods. Cambridge, England: Cambridge University Press, 1968.

Buell, Paul D., *Historical Dictionary of the Mongol World Empire*. Lanham, Md.: The Scarecrow Press, 2003.

Cantor, Norman, Ed., *The Encyclopedia of the Middle Ages*. New York: Viking, 1999.

Carpini, Giovanni DiPlano, Erik Hildinger, Translator, *The Story of the Mongols Whom We Call the Tartars*. Boston: Branden Publishing Company, 1996.

Chambers, James, *The Devil's Horsemen: The Mongol Invasion of Europe* (Reprint of 1979 edition). Edison, N.J.: Castle Books, 2003.

Cleaves, Francis Woodman, Ed. and Translator, *The Secret History of the Mongols*, Volume 1. Cambridge, Mass.: Harvard University Press, 1982.

Fennell, John, *The Crisis of Medieval Russia*, 1200–1304. London: Longman, 1983.

Foltz, Richard C., *Mughal India and Central Asia*. Karachi, India: Oxford University Press, 1998.

"The Gulistan of Sadi." Internet Classics Archive. URL: http://classics.mit.edu/Sadi/gulistan.2.i.html. Accessed December 10, 2003.

Halperin, Charles J., *The Tatar Yoke*. Columbus, Ohio: Slavica Publishers, 1986.

Hodges, Glenn. "Mongolian Crossing." *National Geographic,* Vol. 204, No. 4 (October 2003): 102-121.

Hourani, Albert, *A History of the Arab Peoples*. Cambridge, Mass.: Belknap Press, 1991.

"How Story-telling Began Among Mongols." Mongolia Today Online Magazine. URL: http://www.mongoliatoday.com/issue/7/tales.html. Accessed on December 12, 2003.

James, Peter, and Nick Thorpe, *Ancient Inventions*. New York: Ballantine Books, 1994.

Kwanten, Luc, *Imperial Nomads: A History of Central Asia, 500-1500*. Philadelphia: University of Pennsylvania Press, 1979.

Lawrence, John, *A History of Russia*, 6th ed. New York: New American Library, 1978.

Lee, Sherman, and Wai-Kam Ho, *Chinese Art Under the Mongols: The Yuan Dynasty (1279-1368)*. Cleveland, Ohio: The Cleveland Museum of Art, 1968.

Merriam Webster's Collegiate Dictionary. 10th ed. Springfield, Mass.: Merriam Webster, 1997.

Merriam Webster's Geographical Dictionary. 3rd ed. Springfield, Mass.: Merriam Webster, 1997.

Morgan, David, *The Mongols*. Oxford, England: Blackwell Publishers, 1991.

Nicolle, David, *The Mongol Warlords*. Dorset, England: Firebird Books, 1990.

O'Brien, Patrick K., General ed., *Oxford Atlas of World History*. New York: Oxford University Press, 1999.

Oxford Essential World Atlas. New York: Oxford University Press, 1996.

Pipes. Richard. *Russia Under the Old Regime*. New York: Charles Scribner's Sons, 1974.

Polo, Marco, A.C. Moule, Translator, *The Description of the World*, (Reprint of 1938 edition). New York: AMS Press, 1976.

Polo, Marco, Henry Yule, Translator, Revised translation by Henri Cordier, *The Travels of Marco Polo*, (Reprint of 1903 edition). New York: Dover Publications, 1993.

Polo, Marco, William Marsden, Translator, Manuel Komroff, Ed., *The Travels of Marco Polo*. New York: The Modern Library, 2001.

Raby, Julian, and Teresa Fitzherbert, *The Court of the Il-khans, 1290–1340*. Oxford Studies in Islamic Art XII. Oxford, England: Oxford University Press, 1996.

Ratchnevsky, Paul, Thomas Nivison Haining, Translator and Ed., *Genghis Khan: His Life and Legacy*. Oxford, England: Blackwell Publishers, 1991.

Rossabi, Morris, *Khubilai Khan: His Life and Times*. Berkeley, Calif.: University of California Press, 1988.

Saunders, J.J., *The History of the Mongol Conquests*. Philadelphia: University of Pennsylvania Press, 1971.

Soucek, Svat, *A History of Inner Asia*. Cambridge, England: Cambridge University Press, 2000.

Stewart, Stanley, *In the Empire of Genghis Khan: A Journey Among Nomads*. Guilford, Conn.: The Lyons Press, 2002.

Valadez, Jessica. "Setting the Stage: The Rise of the Yuan Drama, A Culmination of Many Factors." The Yuan Drama. URL: http://www.columbia.edu/~jv287/mongol/drama2.html. Accessed on December 15, 2003.

William of Rubruck, William Woodville Rockhill, Translator and Ed., *The Journey of William of Rubruck to the Eastern Parts of the World, 1253-1255, as Narrated by Himself*. London: The Hakluyt Society, 1900.

INDEX

Page numbers in *italics* refer to illustration captions.